MODEL FLIGHT

MODEL FLIGHT

Martin Simons

NEXUS SPECIAL INTERESTS

Nexus Special Interests Ltd
Nexus House
Boundary Way
Hemel Hempstead
Hertfordshire HP2 7ST
England

First published by Argus Books 1988
Reissued by Nexus Special Interests Ltd, 1998

ISBN 0 85242 938 X

Photosetting by Tradeset Photosetting, Welwyn Garden City.
Printed and bound in Great Britain by
Biddles Ltd, Guildford and King's Lynn

CONTENTS

CHAPTER 3 51
Wing sections

CHAPTER 4 81
The wing in plan

On the cover
Although this book is primarily written for fliers of radio controlled 'conventional' models, it does not ignore other aspects of model flying as exemplified by this *Starduster* free flight contest model by Vince Fazio of Monrovia.   (Photo Ron Moulton).

FOREWORD

It is possible to operate a model aircraft without understanding aerodynamics. Children with paper gliders and simple wooden or plastic models can enjoy themselves without knowledge of the principles of flight. Some adults are content to 'buy and fly' in the same spirit, learning what they need to know as they go along. This is great fun, though without some knowledge of how models fly, the learning process can be long and rather costly.

To fly models one has built oneself is more fun. There is always something to look forward to in the next project and constructing a new model is a most rewarding use of time. Building a model from a kit or a plan usually requires some theoretical knowledge. Without it, important points may be overlooked and the result may be a disappointment. Even the choice of which model to build next depends on some understanding of what different aircraft can do, and how they will fly. Such knowledge helps to avoid accidents.

Perhaps in the longer run the chief reward comes from the added appreciation of what is going on in the air. There is no doubt that people who know what they are doing and why fly better and have more fun than those who operate only by habit or in obedience to some drill.

In this small book, the fundamental principles of flight are explained simply. Neither mathematics nor higher physics is required in order to understand how and why model aircraft behave, and sometimes misbehave, in the way they do. There are many more advanced texts than this, for those who want to go further, but the basic fundamentals explained here should be grasped before resorting to these. Equations and formulae cannot help if the most basic knowledge is lacking.

The ideas explained here are recognised throughout the aviation industry and have been extensively tested and proved in practice. Model fliers who wish, as many have done in the past, to make professional careers in aeronautics should find nothing in this book that will have to be unlearned later.

The book is intended primarily for those who fly 'fixed wing' models under radio control. Very little is said about 'free flight' or control line models, helicopters or other rotorcraft, though ultimately these do operate under the same principles.

For ease of reference, the various sections are numbered according to a decimal system, the first figure indicating the chapter, the figures after the decimal point indicating the section of the chapter. The diagrams are numbered in similar fashion. On almost all occasions, where 'aeroplane' and 'aircraft' appear the words should be taken as referring equally to powered models and gliders and to their full-sized counterparts. Where some distinction has to be made it will be clear from the text.

1   THE BASICS

1.1 Air: a fluid

When an object moves through the atmosphere the air parts, flows around it and closes in behind. If there are any gaps and open passages, the air will flow through. A substance which behaves in this way is a fluid. Air is a mixture of gases and all gases are compressible. Their density, that is, the amount of substance contained in a given space, varies with pressure and temperature.

Liquids like water and oil are also fluids but are hardly compressible at all. They are almost constant in density.

At flight speeds near and above the speed of sound, the compressibility of air becomes very important. Shock waves form. Model aeroplanes do not reach such velocities so compressibility problems do not arise and are not dealt with in this book. Wing shapes and aerofoil sections, fuselage forms and cross-sectional 'area ruling' devised for fast subsonic and supersonic aircraft should not be copied on models unless an exact scale replica is to be built. In this case the performance may be disappointing. It is usually possible to make a scale model of a supersonic aircraft fly even though it is not well shaped for low speed conditions, but flight is sometimes all that can be expected. Scale models of subsonic aeroplanes perform quite well, although models never attain the efficiency of full-sized aircraft. Further discussion of the so-called *scale effect* appears in 3.18.

Variations of atmospheric *density* and *humidity* affect model flight. This is particularly noticeable when models are flown from sites at very high altitudes such as in mountains or on elevated plateaux, and in very hot or very cold weather. Wings and propellers are affected as well as engines. Hence model performance varies a good deal from place to place, season to season and even from day to day. These effects will not be dealt with here in any detail, but they should not be forgotten.

1.2 Aerodynamic reaction

Displacement of the air by a moving body creates resistance which the object feels as a reaction. At a given air density, a large object dis-

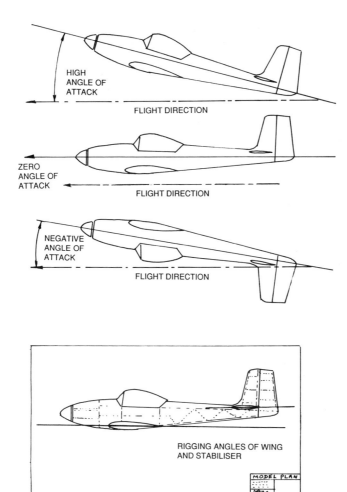

Figure 1.1 Angles of attack and rigging angles

places more air, as it moves, than a small one at the same speed. The large object feels more aerodynamic reaction, other things being equal.

The faster anything moves, the greater the resistance, since more air is disturbed in a given time than with slow movement. Speed has a large influence on all aerodynamic forces. Doubling the velocity of flow produces not twice but four times the reaction.

The shape of anything moving through the air and the angle at which it meets the flow also have great effects on the aerodynamic reactions. The angle at which something lies relative to the direction of its motion through the air is called its *angle of attack,* or, sometimes, its *angle of incidence*. The phrase 'angle of attack' is used here because it always means the angle relative to the air. 'Angle of incidence' sometimes refers to the various angles shown on the plans of the model, to indicate the setting of wing and other surfaces like stabilisers, to some draughtsman's chosen datum or reference line on the paper. These rigging angles do not represent the angle of the surfaces to the airflow. In flight, the angle of attack changes frequently but the lines on the plan remain fixed (Figure 1.1). Angles of incidence may be altered on a model by such tricks as packing up the leading or trailing edges of a wing or stabiliser or, perhaps, by carving away parts of the wing seating, etc. The angle of attack is changed in flight by using the various controls on the model, and may also be altered unexpectedly by turbulence and gusts in the air.

1.3 Streamlined and separated flow

The airflow over and especially behind large, squarish vehicles like buses and heavy goods vans is very irregular. At the rear, swirls and whirls of air called *vortices* form as the air moves in to fill the space. This is a type of *separated* flow. When such large masses of air are violently disturbed, aerodynamic resistance is very great. Much energy is wasted (Figure 1.2).

Vehicles, like aeroplanes, designed to move easily through fluids are shaped so that the flow over them will be as smooth as possible. Such flow is called *streamlined flow*. Preserving the streamlining depends not only on shape but on the angle of attack. An aeroplane is designed for operation within a certain range of angles of attack, the designer assuming that the pilot will keep the angle or *attitude* under control. If the angle of attack becomes too great in any sense, there will be flow separation over large areas, especially on the wings (Figure 1.3). The limits may be exceeded deliberately by the pilot (as sometimes in aerobatics) or accidentally, but the aircraft is not intended to remain outside the designed angle of attack range for very long. When flow separation on the wing becomes general, sustained

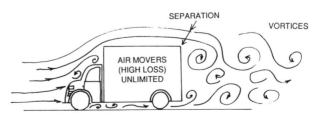

Figure 1.2 Streamlined and separated airflow

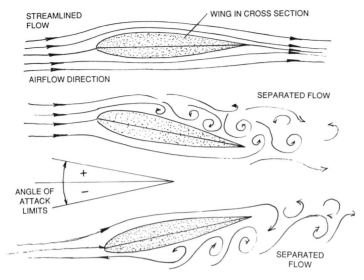

STREAMLINED FLOW

WING IN CROSS SECTION

AIRFLOW DIRECTION

SEPARATED FLOW

ANGLE OF ATTACK LIMITS

+

−

SEPARATED FLOW

Figure 1.3 Streamlined flow will separate (stall)
outside design limits of angle of attack

flight is impossible. A wing which has large areas of flow separation is said to be *stalled*. (See section 1.9 below)

1.4 The aerodynamic centre

Every small part of an aeroplane which has air flowing over it in flight feels a local aerodynamic reaction force. Taking the aircraft as a complete whole, it is possible to add together all such small, local forces to arrive at a single total reaction acting at a single point. The point of action of this total of all aerodynamic forces is called the *aerodynamic centre* of the aircraft. Providing the flow is generally streamlined, that is, the angle of attack is within the designer's limits, the aerodynamic centre is in practice a fixed point. It does not alter its location as the aeroplane changes its position in the air or varies its flight speed etc. The aerodynamic centre is of particular importance when balancing a model in the fore and aft sense, that is, in locating and adjusting the model's *centre of mass* or *centre of gravity*. In working out the stability of an aeroplane, the aerodynamic centre is also frequently termed the *neutral point*. To anticipate the discussion of stability in Chapter 5, it is essential that the centre of gravity of the model should not be further aft than the neutral point (aerodynamic centre) and it should preferably be somewhat ahead of it for a safe model that will be easy to fly.

It is important to remember that the total aerodynamic reaction is found by adding many forces (Figure 1.4). Thus, the total

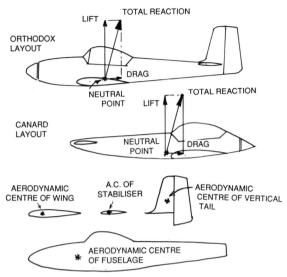

Figure 1.4 The aerodynamic centre or neutral
point of an aircraft is found by adding all forces
at aerodynamic centres of components.
[Note: There is normally an aerodynamic
pitching moment as well as lift and drag.
See section 1.5]

aerodynamic reaction of the wing is found by adding all the small forces on each part of the wing. The sum of these forces acts at the aerodynamic centre of the wing alone. With proper allowance for any taper, sweep or unusual features of the wing outline, this point is always very close to the 25% or quarter chord point, measuring from the leading edge of the mean or average chord. The total aerodynamic force on the fuselage similarly acts at an aerodynamic centre, usually about a quarter of the way along the fuselage, measuring from the nose. The stabiliser (whether foreplane or tailplane), is a small wing with its aerodynamic centre at the 25% mean chord position. Fins are small wings set vertically and a fin too has its aerodynamic centre at 25% mean chord. The same applies to every other part of the aeroplane over which *streamlined* flow of air takes place: wheel spats, struts, etc. The final location of the aerodynamic centre or *neutral point of the entire aircraft* depends on the contribution of each part to the whole. The main wing (or wings) and the horizontal stabiliser are usually the dominant components. (Some models have fin and horizontal stabilisers combined in a 'V' tail arrangement. This makes no difference to the general principles. The effective areas are those found by projection horizontally and vertically.)

The neutral point is almost always found somewhere between the wing and stabiliser on the centre line of the aeroplane, roughly on a line joining the aerodynamic centres of these two major components. Since the wing is larger than the stabiliser, as a rule, the aerodynamic centre (neutral point) of the aircraft is closer to the wing than to the stabiliser, approximately in proportion to their relative areas. This applies to canard or 'tail first' layouts just as it does to the more orthodox wing and tailplane arrangement. If there are several mainplanes, as with biplane, triplane and multiplane aircraft, the aerodynamic centre of the whole set of planes lies on a line joining all their separate aerodynamic centres.

Often on real model aeroplanes there are some local breakdowns of streamlining and areas of separated flow. For instance, when an engine cylinder sticks out into the airflow which cools it, the flow separates behind it. Plump rubber 'airwheels' are not well stream-lined. Control horns, projecting dowels for elastic bands, sharp breaks in the fuselage lines caused by windscreens or cockpit openings, pro-jecting switches, knobs, etc., all cause some separation in their immediate neighbourhood. When two components, such as the wing and fuselage, or a wheel and its supporting strut, join, there is mutual interference and some flow separation often occurs at such places. Fortunately, providing the bulk of the flow over the wings, stabiliser and control surfaces remains attached, small local upsets have very little influence on the aerodynamic centre. Within the designed limits of the angle of attack, the position of this important point remains fixed for practical purposes. The forces acting here vary in both strength and direction as the angle of attack changes through its normal operating range, but the point at which these varying forces act re-mains constant in position. (Many modellers of an older generation find this hard to believe, having been brought up on the theory of a moving *centre of pressure*. This will be explained in Chapter 3 but for the moment these readers are asked to accept that the neutral point is not the same as the centre of pressure.)

1.5 Pitching moments

Most bodies moving freely through the air will not, of their own accord, hold a steady angle of attack to the flow. They tend to pitch or swing one way or the other, depending on their shape. Aerodynamic *pitch-ing moments* of this kind tend to change the angle of attack. Part of the aerodynamic reaction, when all forces are added at the neutral point of an aeroplane, is therefore a total pitching moment resulting from the pitching tendencies of wings, fuselage, undercarriage, etc. The wing, as usual, is a dominant component in this.

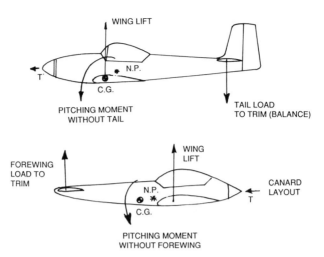

Figure 1.5 Balancing the pitching moments
For flight in any constant attitude (level, diving, climbing, etc.),
the aircraft must be *trimmed*. This usually requires the
stabiliser to be set at a suitable angle of attack so that
the *total* of all pitching forces is zero.

Other pitching forces arise from the moment of the weight of the model, acting at the centre of gravity. The propeller and thrust force also produce pitching moments.

For any given position, level, diving, climbing, turning, inverted flight, etc., all such forces must be brought to balance. This is normally achieved by using the controls to 'trim' the pitching moments to zero. In the fore and aft or longitudinal sense, the stabiliser and elevator are the crucial control surfaces which accomplish this (Figure 1.5).

1.6 Lift and drag

Flight of 'heavier than air' craft depends on using aerodynamic reactions to support the weight of the vehicle. The mainplanes normally provide the bulk of the support although if the thrust axis (of propeller or jet reaction motor) is inclined upwards, the wing is relieved of some of its load. (In a vertical climb, all the support comes from the thrust, but a propeller is a rotating wing system. Rotorcraft gain all their support from the aerodynamic reactions on their rotating wings.)

Any part of the total reaction which cannot be converted into upward support or *lift* remains as *drag*, which resists the motion. The lift and drag are both derived from the total aerodynamic reaction and both act at the aerodynamic centre (neutral point) of the aeroplane (Figure 1.6). It is because the wing is by far the most important generator of aerodynamic reaction that the neutral point is nearer to

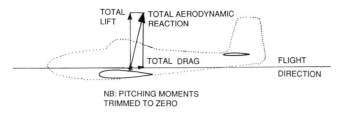

NB: PITCHING MOMENTS
TRIMMED TO ZERO

Figure 1.6 The origin of lift and drag

the wing, but the stabiliser, a small wing, may provide some lift force and this must be taken into account (Figure 1.5).

The wing also creates a great deal of drag. Wing drag nearly always amounts to more than half the total drag of an aeroplane. Wing drag is an inevitable price that has to be paid for lift and cannot be avoided although it may be reduced by good design. The rest of the aeroplane, fuselage, fins, undercarriage (if not retracted), engine cooling arrangements, struts, etc., create drag without making much, if any, contribution to the total lift. This drag, for which there is no pay-off in terms of supporting force, is commonly termed *parasite* or *parasitic drag.*

The stabiliser creates drag which is usually included in the parasitic drag total. This component's contribution to the total lift is always small. On an orthodox aeroplane or glider, with a tailplane, the tail 'lift' load is usually downwards (Figure 1.5), although as the aircraft is controlled by the pilot to fly at different angles of attack, the tail may sometimes be required to act upwards. When the stabiliser 'lifts' downwards, this force must be added to the total downward load and accordingly, the wing is required to produce some additional support. With a well-designed aircraft, the quantities involved are quite small. The advantage often claimed for the canard layout is that, unlike a tailplane, the forewing contributes to the total upward supporting force, so that there is some reward for the drag of this item. There are disadvantages in this layout which tend to offset the gains.

The lift component of the total aerodynamic force always acts at right angles to the direction of flight and the drag always directly downstream. This remains true whatever position the aeroplane may take with respect to the ground. For instance, in a steep dive the direction of flight is inclined down (Figure 1.7). The lift force is still at right angles to the flight path and the drag directly backwards against the motion. Climbing flight finds the same rules operating.

Aeroplanes may be trimmed to fly either 'nose up' or 'nose down' in level flight. At maximum speed under power, the angle of attack will

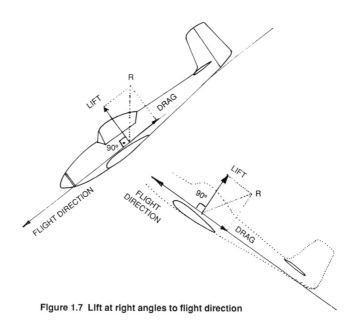

Figure 1.7 Lift at right angles to flight direction

be small and the model will appear 'nose down', but at slow speed the angle of attack will be greater, 'nose up', even though the flight path remains level. The lift force is always at right angles to the flight direction and the drag always directly backwards, even as the angle of attack to the airflow changes rapidly during manoeuvres, aerobatics, etc.

In turning flight when the model is banked over to one side or the other, the lift force acts at right angles to the wing, i.e., it is tilted by the same amount as the bank angle.

1.7 The lift:drag ratio

The amount of lift a wing can provide depends on its size, measured in terms of *total area*, its *speed* through the air, its *aerofoil section* or *profile* and *angle of attack*.

In level flight (ignoring any small stabiliser loads) the total lift and total weight are equal (Figure 1.8). It is interesting to know how much drag is produced by the aircraft, in relation to the weight supported. The drag resists the motion and has to be overcome by a forward driving force: thrust in the case of a powered model. To know how much drag a model creates at some particular flight velocity is to know how much thrust force it needs to maintain flight at this speed. Since lift equals weight in level flight trim, and drag equals thrust, the ratio of lift to drag, lift/drag or L/D is the same as the ratio of weight to thrust. A

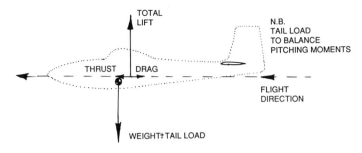

Figure 1.8 In level flight; Lift ≈ Weight; Thrust = Drag

high L/D indicates that the thrust required to maintain a given weight of aircraft in level flight is low, the aircraft is efficient. A low L/D indicates the reverse. The more efficient an aeroplane is, the faster it will fly on a given power.

Ignoring fuel consumption, the mass of a model is constant. So, in level flight with the trim and throttle adjusted for a variety of speeds, the lift remains the same as the weight, but the drag changes with the angle of attack. At some particular angle of attack the drag will be at its least possible value. This trim will then yield the most efficient or *maximum L/D* value for the particular aeroplane (Figure 1.9).

With gliders the driving force is obtained by tilting the flight path slightly downwards to use the force of gravity, very much as a skier slides down a snow covered slope. The L/D ratio of a sailplane is closely related to the angle of glide. A low L/D ratio requires a steeper glide to keep the driving force up to the required value. A high L/D indicates a shallow glide (Figure 1.10). Full-sized sailplanes in the open class (unrestricted as to size, weight, cost etc.) achieve best L/D ratios of 50/1, i.e., their drag at best L/D trim is only one fiftieth of their total weight. A 50/1 L/D indicates that, in still air, a sailplane could travel 50 metres horizontally for each metre of height lost. Putting this another way, if such a sailplane is on tow behind an aeroplane in level flight, when accurately flown at the best L/D angle of attack, the force in the tow rope pulling the glider along will be one fiftieth of the sailplane's total weight. A 500 kg sailplane can therefore be towed with a 10 kg force in the rope. (The ropes actually used are much stronger. Starting from standstill on the ground, gusts in flight, and mishandling by either pilot increase the rope strains greatly. Note also that the best trim for soaring flight, as distinct from distance gliding, is at a slower airspeed than the best L/D, at a flight speed which gives the minimum rate of sink.) Alternatively such a sailplane could just be kept aloft by a small motor capable of giving 10 kg thrust. (Gaining height is a different story.)

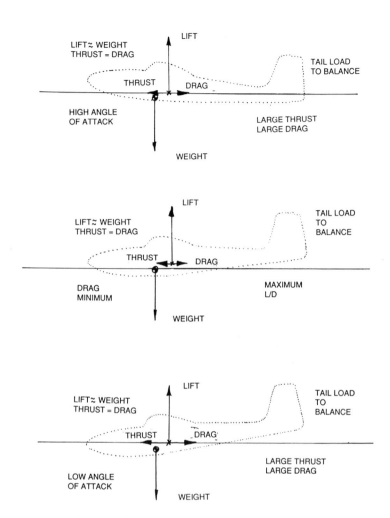

Figure 1.9 The meaning of the lift:drag ratio; Weight:Thrust

Model sailplanes, because of scale effects, rarely reach L/D ratios better than 30/1.

Powered model aeroplanes are usually much less efficient and maximum L/D ratios of 8/1 are probably about average. It is not always desirable to have a very high L/D ratio. The highly efficient model will tend to float long distances just above the ground when landing, making judgment of the touch down point very difficult. In dives, an efficient aircraft picks up speed very quickly, which can lead to trouble. For these reasons, although experienced pilots prefer aircraft with relatively high L/D ratios, for beginners and 'sport' pilots a

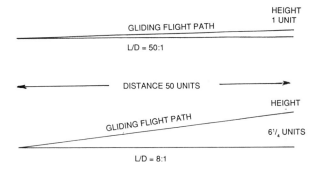

HEIGHT
1 UNIT

GLIDING FLIGHT PATH

L/D = 50:1

DISTANCE 50 UNITS

HEIGHT

GLIDING FLIGHT PATH

6¼ UNITS

L/D = 8:1

Figure 1.10 The relationship of L/D ratio to gliding

less efficient aeroplane is often more satisfactory. The landing problem with high L/D aircraft like sailplanes is often solved by using spoilers, airbrakes or landing flaps which increase the drag, so steepening the descent path and making judgment of the touchdown point much easier.

1.8 Thrust, drag and speed

As mentioned above, when a powered model is flying straight and level at some speed, the thrust equals the total drag. If the drag can be reduced, for instance by retracting the undercarriage, while the thrust is unchanged, the model will accelerate (Figure 1.11). Since all aerodynamic forces increase as the speed of flow increases (twice the speed means four times the aerodynamic reaction), as the speed rises the drag becomes more until it once again equals the thrust. If the power is then increased, by opening the throttle of the motor for instance, the model will again accelerate but the drag will soon catch up and come to equal the thrust at its new value. When the thrust is at its maximum and all possible means of reducing drag have been used, the model will reach its maximum speed in level flight. To move any faster relative to the air requires additional driving force to aid the thrust. This can be achieved by diving, to use gravity, but again, as the model speeds up in the dive, the drag rises rapidly and again comes to equal the total driving force, thrust plus gravitational influence. In a truly vertical dive (from a very great height), the thrust of the engine plus the total weight of the model combine. The speed rises but the drag soon catches up and the maximum possible velocity or *terminal velocity* is reached when the drag equals the thrust plus weight forces. (Needless to say, few models achieve a terminal velocity dive since they usually hit the ground before the maximum possible speed is reached.)

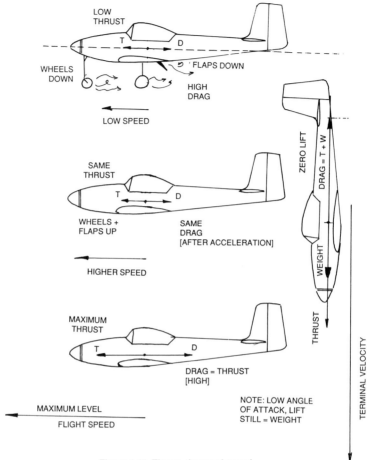

LOW
THRUST

T D

WHEELS
DOWN

FLAPS DOWN

HIGH
DRAG

LOW SPEED

SAME
THRUST

T D

WHEELS +
FLAPS UP

SAME
DRAG
[AFTER ACCELERATION]

HIGHER SPEED

MAXIMUM
THRUST

T D

DRAG = THRUST
[HIGH]

MAXIMUM LEVEL

FLIGHT SPEED

NOTE: LOW ANGLE
OF ATTACK, LIFT
STILL = WEIGHT

ZERO LIFT

DRAG = T + W

WEIGHT

THRUST

TERMINAL VELOCITY

Figure 1.11 Thrust, drag and speed

1.9 Pitching moments of wings

How powerful the pitching moment of wings, and wing-like forms such as fins and stabilisers, are depends chiefly on their cross sectional shape or profile. Wings which are not symmetrical in cross section have an inherent and inevitable tendency to pitch to a different angle of attack (Figure 1.12). The only exception is the 'reflex' type of wing profile, described in 3.8. *Symmetrical profile shapes have zero pitching moments.* As long as the airflow over them is not separated, they do not tend to pitch either to lower or higher angles of attack. On the other hand, if they are disturbed by something like a gust, they do not tend to return to their original position. They are *neutral* with respect to flight direction, putting up no resistance to change. Even though the

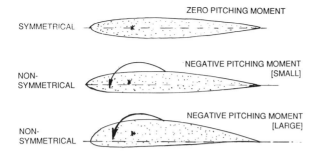

Figure 1.12 The negative [nose down]
pitching moment of aerofoils

pitching moment is zero, the lift of a symmetrical sectioned wing varies if the angle of attack is allowed to wander, and if it takes up too large an angle under the influence of accidental disturbances, a stall will occur just as it will with any other wing.

1.10 Stalling

At some high angle of attack the airflow over the wing will separate. In this condition the aerodynamic reaction changes dramatically. Lift decreases and drag increases. The wing pitching moment in the nose down sense also increases very sharply. This type of drastic flow separation is *stalling* and the angle at which it occurs is the *stalling angle* (Figure 1.13). To restore the flow, the angle of attack must be decreased to bring it back within the design limits. The large increase in negative pitching moment helps to achieve this. After a stall, most models will automatically rotate sharply in the nose down direction and enter a dive.

In inverted flight, there is an inverted stalling angle.

Pilots may stall their aircraft deliberately in aerobatics or at the moment of touch down. An unintentional stall may be caused by turbulence in the air or by a piloting error. The sudden loss of lift causes a correspondingly sharp loss of height together with the abrupt nose-down pitching motion. In all cases, whether the stall is intentional or not, it is important to retain control of the angle of attack so that attached flow can be restored at the pilot's command.

Stalling is entirely a matter of the angle of attack, not the speed of flight. Whatever the speed, if the angle of attack to the airflow is too great, the flow will separate. What is often referred to as the *stalling speed* is only the minimum possible flying speed for the aircraft when it is flying with engine throttled fully back and the angle of attack is just at the stalling angle. When landing, the touch down should, ideally,

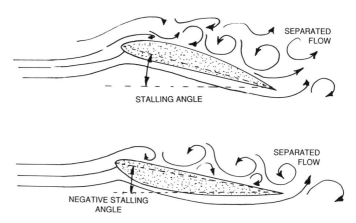

STALLING ANGLE

NEGATIVE STALLING ANGLE

SEPARATED FLOW

Figure 1.13 The stalling angle

occur just at the moment of this low speed stall, so that the landing run will be short. Models may be fitted with various devices, such as flaps, to reduce their stalling speed for landing. But if the stalling angle is reached at some higher speed, the wing will stall. This *high speed stall* is a common cause of accidents in pylon racing, since during the very steep turns required to round the pylons, the wing is called upon to operate at high angles of attack and it is easy to exceed the stalling angle, usually with disastrous results.

By careful design of the wing aerofoil section and by wise layout of the wing planform (the view of the wing from directly above) it is possible to reduce the danger of accidental stalling. A mild stall is one in which the airflow begins to separate gradually, near the centre of the wing, and spreads out sideways fairly slowly. This may be sensed and corrected early before it affects the whole wing from tip to tip. A stall which occurs suddenly across the entire wing span can catch even an experienced pilot by surprise. If the stall begins at the wing tips and spreads inwards from there, a very dangerous condition can arise because what nearly always happens is that one tip stalls before the other and the wing on that side loses much of its lift while the other is not yet stalled. The model rolls sharply to one side before the pilot can correct it. This is most likely to happen during the slow approach to land, or just after take off, and when it does so, an accident is almost certain.

1.11 'G' forces

In manoeuvres such as turns, pulling out of dives, and in most aerobatics, the load on the aircraft is increased by centrifugal forces, which must be resisted. 'G' forces arise (Figure 1.14). In negative man-

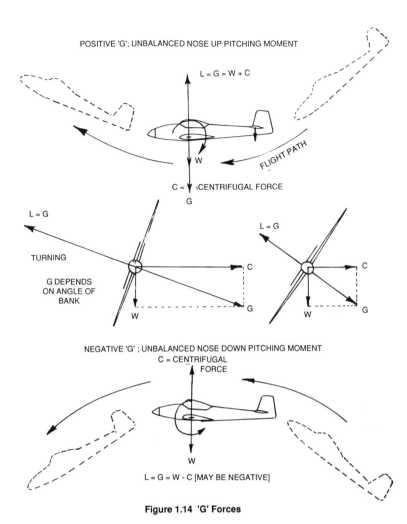

POSITIVE 'G'; UNBALANCED NOSE UP PITCHING MOMENT

L = G = W + C

W

C = ↓ (CENTRIFUGAL FORCE

G

L = G

TURNING

G DEPENDS
ON ANGLE OF
BANK

FLIGHT PATH

L = G

C

W

G

L = G

C

W

G

NEGATIVE 'G' ; UNBALANCED NOSE DOWN PITCHING MOMENT

C = CENTRIFUGAL
FORCE

W

L = G = W - C [MAY BE NEGATIVE]

Figure 1.14 'G' Forces

oeuvres such as bunts (nosing down from level flight into the inverted position), outside loops, etc., the 'G' force is negative (reversed). It is often necessary to make model wings strong and stiff enough to withstand five or six 'G', that is, five or six times the normal load of level flight, in both the up and down, or positive and negative, directions. A safety factor is usually added to this to allow for defects in workmanship or materials. Flight in turbulent air can also have a multiplying effect on loads; for instance, an aeroplane in the midst of an aerobatic programme may strike a severe gust just at the moment when the wings are near their maximum allowable stress. This will increase the loads on the wings and may break them.

2   THE CONTROLS

2.1 The control axes

It is usual, in discussing the controllability, trim and stability of an aircraft, to employ a reference system of three axes, X, Y and Z, which are assumed to pass through the *centre of gravity* or *balance point* of the aeroplane (Figure 2.1).

The *X axis* runs more or less from nose to tail but is not necessarily aligned with the thrust axis or even parallel to it. For convenience the X axis is often drawn on the plans of the model as a datum line parallel to the supposed direction of flight at some chosen trim and flight speed, but as the trim and power vary during a flight, this nominal alignment does not hold. Since the axes are fixed relative to the aircraft, when the model is flying level slowly, nose up, the X axis is canted upwards and when flying fast, it is canted downwards. At some intermediate trim and speed, perhaps the 'cruising' trim, it may be parallel with the flight path.

The crosswise or *Y axis* runs from side to side at right angles to the X axis and parallel to the line joining the wing tips. It may not pass through the tips unless these happen to be exactly in line with the centre of gravity in side view.

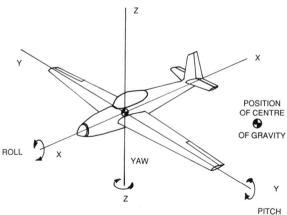

Figure 2.1 The three axes

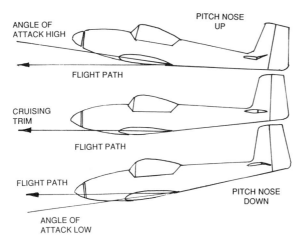

ANGLE OF
ATTACK HIGH

PITCH NOSE
UP

FLIGHT PATH

CRUISING
TRIM

FLIGHT PATH

FLIGHT PATH

PITCH NOSE
DOWN

ANGLE OF
ATTACK LOW

Figure 2.2 Angle of attack control

The vertical *Z axis* runs at right angles to the other two in the vertical plane.

Rotations including *pitching* motions, nose up, nose down, rolling motions, banking the wing to either side and *yawing*, the nose swinging from side to side, are regarded as being centred on the various axes and since these pass through the centre of gravity, all such motions are referred to the c.g. as the point for measurements of trim and balance. In flight the controls are used to rotate the aircraft about the various axes and to hold any desired attitude. Most problems of control and stability arise because the aerodynamic forces act as if concentrated at the neutral point while gravity acts on the mass of the model at the centre of balance. These two points rarely coincide. As mentioned in Chapter 1, the c.g. is placed ahead of the neutral point for safe flight and pitching moments are balanced out by the stabilisers. Each movement of the controls changes the balance, causing a rotation about one or more of the axes, with a new balance and new flight attitude to be established thereafter. The relationship of c.g. and neutral point is a critical factor. Most problems of control can be solved by adjusting the c.g.

2.2 Control in pitch

Control in pitch, that is, rotation around the crosswise or Y axis, involves changes of the angle of attack of the mainplane.

The angle of attack is, as always, measured relative to the direction of flight, not relative to the ground or any horizontal line (Figure 2.2).

At a given flight speed, an increase in the angle of attack causes an increase of the lift force and the model accelerates up relative to its own reference system. If the angle of attack is reduced, the decrease of lift force produces a negative acceleration. All such accelerations are resisted by mass inertia acting at the centre of gravity.

Control of the mainplane's angle of attack, i.e., rotation about the Y axis, is thus crucial for all manoeuvres in the up and down sense. This applies not only to changes from level flight to diving or climbing attitudes, loops and inverted loops, but also to turning flight. In a turn, the force needed to move the aircraft laterally (sideways) is obtained by tilting, or banking, the wing so that some of the *wing lift force* turns the model. Relative to the aircraft, this is an upward acceleration as well as a lateral movement (Figure 2.3), and is resisted. as usual, by inertia acting at the centre of gravity against the turn.

To change the angle of attack, it is usual to employ an *elevator* (Figure 2.4). The most common form of elevator is a hinged surface which also forms part of the horizontal stabiliser. Sailplanes commonly have stabilisers which are 'all moving' and so act as elevators, but the principle is the same. Altering the elevator angle changes the lift load on the whole of the stabiliser and this change in balance (trim) causes the model to rotate about the Y axis, to a different angle of attack. If, as is usually the case, the tailplane carries a down load, lowering the elevator *decreases but does not reverse* this download, so

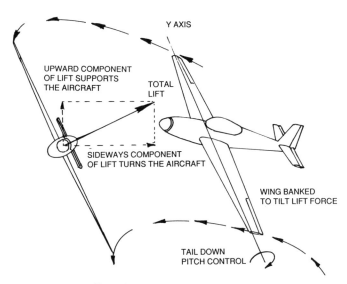

Figure 2.3 Pitch control in turning flight.
During a turn, the aircraft constantly pitches
tail down around the crosswise Y axis

the balance is changed in a nose down sense. Raising the elevator increases the download, causing a nose up rotation (the other way round for a canard). Hence, a down elevator position does not imply that the load on the tail is upwards (Figure 2.5). It is usually just less downwards than before. In a dive, with elevator down, the load on the tailplane of an orthodox model is still downwards and as the speed rises the actual force involved is large. (Twice the speed means four times the aerodynamic force.) Tailplanes bend and sometimes break downwards when models are diving.

If the model is inverted, moving the control column back (up elevator) rotates the model in the same sense as when it is upright, but since it is upside down the nose drops relative to the ground (and the airspeed normally increases).

It is possible to achieve control of angle of attack by other means than the usual elevator arrangement (Figure 2.6). Hinged flaps on the

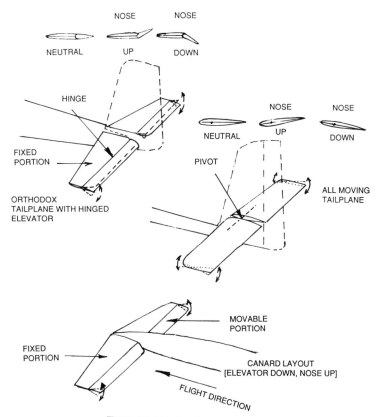

Figure 2.4 The elevator

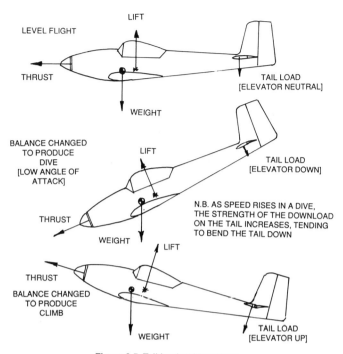

Figure 2.5 Tail loads with various
elevator positions. [See also Fig. 1.5]

trailing edge of the mainplane may be used. On 'tailless' or 'flying wing' aircraft such flaps are commonly employed as elevators. Some aeroplanes have flown successfully with a fixed stabiliser and a variable incidence wing which pivots as a whole, under the pilot's command. This achieves the same result, a pitching rotation about the Y axis and hence a change of angle of attack. There are considerable difficulties in making an entire wing pivot in this way. The orthodox elevator is much simpler and lighter, so the variable incidence wing system, although satisfactory from the aerodynamic viewpoint, is very rarely used because of the engineering problems.

The relationship of the thrust line on the model to the centre of gravity affects the angle of attack if the thrust varies. As mentioned above (1.5), pitching moments due to the thrust are normally balanced out by the tail or forewing loads, but if the thrust line passes above the c.g., when the power increases there is an increase in nose down pitching moments. A decrease in power reduces the nose down pitching forces. Conversely, if the thrust line passes below the c.g., increases of power tend to pitch the nose up and decreases have the opposite effect. The position of the thrust line cannot normally be

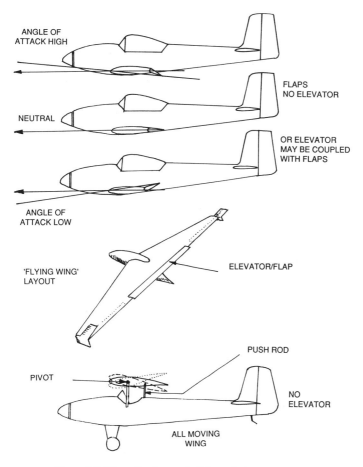

ANGLE OF
ATTACK HIGH

FLAPS
NO ELEVATOR

NEUTRAL

OR ELEVATOR
MAY BE COUPLED
WITH FLAPS

ANGLE OF
ATTACK LOW

'FLYING WING'
LAYOUT

ELEVATOR/FLAP

PUSH ROD

PIVOT

NO
ELEVATOR

ALL MOVING
WING

Figure 2.6 Alternative forms of pitch control

altered during flight, but can be adjusted by modifying the engine mountings or by inserting washers and spacers under the engine flanges when bolting the power unit in place. Such dodges actually have small effects unless carried to extremes. Model fliers sometimes worry unnecessarily about these adjustments, adding 'downthrust' and 'upthrust' to try to achieve better trim, but finding that the effects are often almost negligible in practice.

As discussed further below (2.5), changes of power in flight cause considerable changes in pitching moments because each power variation alters the *flight speed,* and this is a much more powerful influence on pitching control than thrust line position.

It is also possible to achieve control in pitch by moving the centre of gravity back or forward, by means of movable ballast weights, or, as is sometimes done in full-sized flying, by pumping fuel from tanks in the rear of the aircraft to tanks in front, or vice versa. Passengers moving about inside airliners also alter the trim in pitch, though such effects are small relative to the total mass of the aircraft unless all crowd into the rear, or rush to the front together (a practice discouraged by airline operators). Some sailplanes have liquid mercury with pumps to move it between reservoirs fore and aft, to allow centre of gravity trimming for different flight conditions.

The various alternative control systems have serious disadvantages which make the ordinary elevator control almost universal. It is sometimes worthwhile, especially on aerobatic aircraft which are required to perform 'square' manoeuvres with very sharp changes of pitch, to combine elevator and wing flaps to achieve very large lift changes of the mainplane, but on almost all other occasions, the elevator is perfectly adequate.

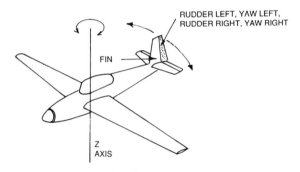

Figure 2.7 The rudder

2.3 Control in yaw

Control in yaw, rotation about the vertical or Z axis, is almost invariably achieved by using a *rudder* or several rudders. A rudder may be hinged to a fin, forming part of the vertical stabilising surface (Figure 2.7). Moving the rudder changes the cross section of the whole vertical surface and the resulting forces are thus much greater than those on the rudder itself. All-moving rudders are sometimes used and there is no necessity for the rudder to be associated directly with the fin. On magnet steered hill soaring gliders, for instance, a small fin at the tail is often used, with an all-moving rudder surface at the nose, where the magnet apparatus is fitted.

Yawing is not turning (Figure 2.8). Aeroplanes are not like boats which use rudders as the primary turning control, because in flight an aircraft does not necessarily follow its nose. To provide a force capable of turning an aircraft it is necessary to tilt or bank the wing, as has been mentioned above. The wing lift turns the model (Figure 2.3).

Some model aircraft, especially trainers and thermal soaring sailplanes, do rely on the rudder for turning, but what the rudder does in these cases is *to cause the wing to bank*. Yawing the model has the *secondary effect* of banking the wing over and the *wing lift* then turns the model. The bank occurs when the rudder is applied because the wing is set at a fairly generous *dihedral angle*. (That is, when viewed from the front, the tips of the wing are higher than the roots. Figure 2.9.) A yaw, caused by the rudder, forces the model to present one wing to the air at a greater angle of attack than the other (See Chapter 5, sections 5.9 & 10). This causes the lift on one side to increase and

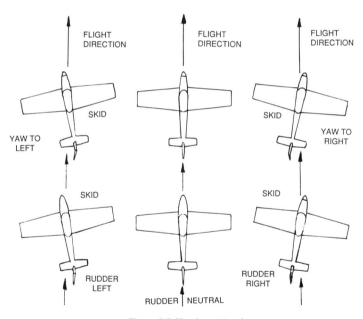

Figure 2.8 Yaw is not turning

so tilt the aircraft and start the turn. If the wing has insufficient dihedral, the rudder action fails as a turning control. The model will yaw when the rudder is applied but there will be very slight or nil turning effect because the wing is not banked.

A tall rudder extending well above the rolling axis of the aircraft actually causes a small rolling force opposing the turn, although with normal layouts this is hardly appreciable.

The rudder is important mainly to keep the aircraft aligned with the flow direction despite the various forces which arise tending to cause

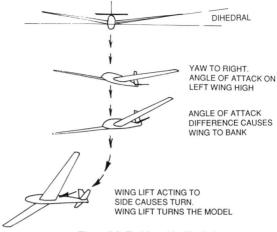

DIHEDRAL

YAW TO RIGHT.
ANGLE OF ATTACK ON
LEFT WING HIGH

ANGLE OF ATTACK
DIFFERENCE CAUSES
WING TO BANK

WING LIFT ACTING TO
SIDE CAUSES TURN.
WING LIFT TURNS THE MODEL

Figure 2.9 Rudder with dihedral as
a method of turning

a misalignment. For the wing to provide lift, for example, it is necessary for the air to flow more or less from front to rear, rather than sideways from tip to tip, and the yawing control is there to assure this. If
the fuselage is yawed, the airflow over it will separate, creating much
drag. (This may be useful if it is desired to sideslip the model.)

In aerobatics, the yawing action of the rudder is used in some rolling
and 'knife edged' manoeuvres, to tilt the thrust line at times when the
wings are vertically banked and cannot provide their usual upward
force (Figure 2.10).

When the rudder and fin are within the *slipstream* from the model's
propeller, the increased flow velocity multiplies the aerodynamic
forces on these vertical surfaces and they become more effective and
more sensitive. (Figure 2.11. The same is true of the horizontal
stabiliser and elevator if these lie within the slipstream.) On models
where the vertical stabiliser and rudder do not benefit from any
slipstream, as with all gliders and some powered aircraft where the

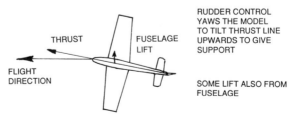

THRUST

FUSELAGE
LIFT

FLIGHT
DIRECTION

RUDDER CONTROL
YAWS THE MODEL
TO TILT THRUST LINE
UPWARDS TO GIVE
SUPPORT

SOME LIFT ALSO FROM
FUSELAGE

Figure 2.10 'Knife edge' flight. With vertical
bank, no wing lift is available

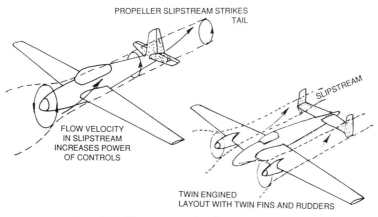

PROPELLER SLIPSTREAM STRIKES TAIL

FLOW VELOCITY IN SLIPSTREAM INCREASES POWER OF CONTROLS

SLIPSTREAM

TWIN ENGINED LAYOUT WITH TWIN FINS AND RUDDERS

Figure 2.11 Slipstream velocity effects on control power

layout ensures the slipstream misses these surfaces, effectiveness is much reduced and accordingly rudder and fin have to be increased in size to compensate. The effect is also noticeable on some powered models when the engine is throttled back or cut, since the slipstream is no longer effective and rudder control suffers. Models with twin engines and single, central fins may lack rudder power. They can overcome this by being fitted with twin vertical tails, the rudders then lying behind the two propellers and within the slipstream. Failure of one engine may still produce a critical situation since total rudder power will be reduced at a time when the asymmetrical power produces strong yawing forces.

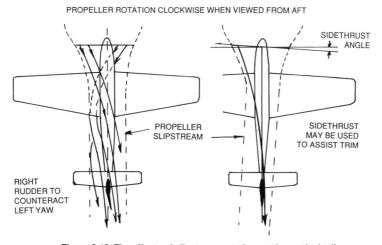

PROPELLER ROTATION CLOCKWISE WHEN VIEWED FROM AFT

SIDETHRUST ANGLE

PROPELLER SLIPSTREAM

SIDETHRUST MAY BE USED TO ASSIST TRIM

RIGHT RUDDER TO COUNTERACT LEFT YAW

Figure 2.12 The effects of slipstream rotation on the vertical tail

Because the propeller slipstream rotates, the vertical tail almost always lies in a region of airflow which is not directly fore and aft (Figure 2.12). This tends to yaw the aeroplane and some rudder offset or trim to one side is often required to counteract this. Many full-sized, propeller driven aircraft, such as piston engined fighters before and during World War 2, with very large propellers and powerful motors, used to have vertical fins offset or cambered slightly to provide a continuous balancing force against the yaw caused by the slipstream. The engine may be mounted at a small angle of 'sidethrust', to achieve a similar effect.

The other most important duty of the rudder and vertical stabiliser is to enable the model to recover from spins or, in aerobatics, to enter them and recover. More on this topic is said below (2.13).

2.4 Control in roll

As stressed above, turning an aeroplane requires the wing to be banked over so that the lift produces a lateral force to move the aircraft sideways (Figure 2.3). Attempting to turn a model with the wing flat is not merely ineffective but also very inefficient, since it causes very large increases in drag. A *correctly flown turn is always a banked turn,* the steeper the angle of bank, the greater the rate of turn. The roll control is thus a primary turning control. Since, when the wing is banked, the lift force is not acting directly upwards relative to the ground, it is always necessary to compensate for this by increasing the angle of attack at the same time as banking the model. The total wing lift force then can provide both the lateral force and the required upward force to support the weight (See also Figure 1.14). Turning efficiently therefore is always a matter of co-ordinating the roll control with the

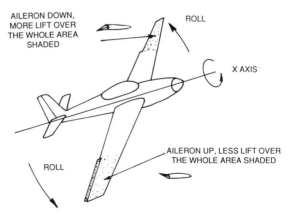

AILERON DOWN, MORE LIFT OVER THE WHOLE AREA SHADED

ROLL

X AXIS

AILERON UP, LESS LIFT OVER THE WHOLE AREA SHADED

ROLL

Figure 2.13 Ailerons for control of roll

elevator. Meanwhile, any tendency to yaw out of line with the airflow should be counteracted with the rudder.

Control in roll, rotation arond the X axis, is achieved by making the wing on one side of the aeroplane lift more strongly than on the other. Here again, various devices are possible and most have been tried at some time or other on model and full-sized aeroplanes.

Ailerons achieve control in roll by modifying the cross section of the wing. Drooping an aileron converts the wing into a more *cambered* form (see Chapter 3), so increasing the lift force. On the other side of the aircraft, the other aileron is raised, reducing the camber and lift, and the result is a roll. The effect of the aileron is to change the aerodynamic force over the whole part of the wing which lies ahead of the hinge line (Figure 2.13). Aileron power is therefore much greater than might be thought, and long, narrow ailerons, extending across a large proportion of the wing span, are generally much more effective than short, relatively broad ones which change the camber over only a small part of the wing. If a model has insufficient control in the rolling plane, it is usually much better to increase the length of the ailerons than to make them wider in chord.

Unfortunately, any increase of lift on a part of a wing increases the drag. More on this appears in Chapter 4, but for the moment it is only necessary to recognise that ailerons always create extra drag on the wing which is to be raised. The drag on the other wing is reduced simultaneously. The result is that a roll is accompanied by an *adverse yaw* (Figure 2.14). The upgoing wing is dragged backwards. Adverse yaw caused by the ailerons is opposed by the fin and rudder.

A common device is to gear the ailerons differentially, so that the aileron on one side droops only slightly, or not at all, as the other one

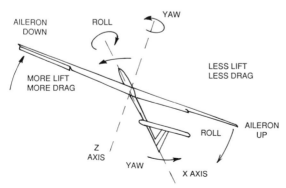

Figure 2.14 Adverse yaw in turns caused by
unequal lift on wings

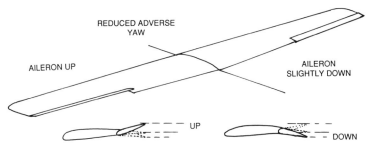

Figure 2.15 Differential ailerons

rises (Figure 2.15). This is only slightly effective in reducing the adverse yaw, which is caused by the fundamental difference in lift on the two wings. This difference is necessary in order to achieve the roll, and some adverse effect is inevitable, however the ailerons are geared. Differential ailerons are fairly effective for aircraft which tend to fly mostly at low speeds and high angles of attack, such as thermal soaring sailplanes and scale models of slow flying, veteran and vintage aeroplanes.

Instead of ailerons, the entire wing can be pivoted at the root, so that at the pilot's will one side can be set at a greater angle than the other (Figure 2.16). Variations on this have involved rotating wing tip panels. Such devices are effective aerodynamically, but like the variable incidence wing tend to introduce structural complications. The wing root is an area where structural loads are high and to carry these loads through a system of rotating pivots is not easy. Pivoting wings and rotating wing tips are also prone to *flutter* dangerously at high speeds, unless very carefully balanced and firmly mounted. These devices do not overcome the adverse yaw characteristics of ailerons, since they rely on making one wing operate at a higher angle of attack than the other, with consequent drag imbalance tending to yaw the model away from the turn. Powerful rudder action is required.

Control in roll may also be accomplished by using *spoilers* on the wing, hinged plates which can be raised on one side or the other, disturbing the streamlined flow in their neighbourhood and so reducing the lift. They also increase the drag on one side which may actually be of help. The drag of the spoiler tends to yaw the aircraft into the direction of the turn, as if the rudder were applied in that direction. Such spoilers are often found on full-sized jet aircraft in combination with ailerons but they are rarely used as the primary roll control. They have the disadvantage of uneven response. Opening the spoiler slightly has very little effect. If it is opened a little more, it may suddenly cause the flow to break away with a sharp 'grab', but further opening produces only slight increase in response. Such a control tends to be 'all or nothing' and does not make for smooth flight.

Spoilers and ailerons may be coupled so that as the aileron goes up and the wing goes down, the spoiler on the same side rises to provide the corrective yawing force.

2.5 Trimming

Every controlled change in flight attitude may be thought of in three phases: (1) The controls are moved to *initiate a rotation* about one or more of the control axes. (2) The rotation has to be *checked* by control action the other way. (3) A *new trim* is established. It is an unusual coincidence if the first two actions put the controls in exactly the right position to hold the new trim. With experience, the pilot becomes so familiar with the three phases of control initiation, check and then re-trimming, that they run together and become virtually one instinctive movement.

For instance, if a certain angle of bank, corresponding to a given rate of turn, is wanted, the ailerons are first moved to initiate the roll, while the rudder is used as required to counteract any adverse yaw (Phase 1). The roll is checked by a counter action (Phase 2). Then a new aileron position is found so that the desired bank and turn is held (Phase 3). With most powered models the ailerons will be centralised once a particular angle of bank is established. With sailplanes it is almost always the case that the final trimmed position will need the ailerons to be set slightly *against* the turn. This *hold off bank* is neces-

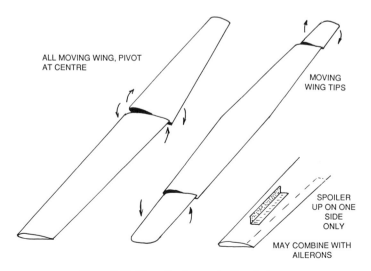

ALL MOVING WING, PIVOT
AT CENTRE

MOVING
WING TIPS

SPOILER
UP ON ONE
SIDE
ONLY

MAY COMBINE WITH
AILERONS

Figure 2.16 Alternative forms of roll control

sary because of the influence of flow speed on aerodynamic forces. In a turn, the inner wing of a large span sailplane is moving more slowly through the air than the outer wing. The angle of attack of the inner wing is slightly greater than that of the outer wing, but the flow speed difference, caused by the large span, is more than enough to overcome this. The inner wing produces less lift than the other one, so if the ailerons are held neutral, the model will tend to roll more into the turn. To prevent this and keep the rate of turn constant, the pilot has to apply a little aileron the other way. This becomes automatic with practice. The pilot flies the aircraft by watching its behaviour carefully, moving the controls to whatever settings they have to take to maintain the desired attitude.

If, from level flight, the pilot wishes the model to climb, the nose is first pitched up by the elevator, increasing the angle of attack (Phase 1). The rotation is checked when the desired angle of attack is reached, by a forward elevator stick movement (Phase 2). The increase of lift causes the model to move upwards but as it does so, the airspeed tends to slow down. To ascend against gravitational attraction requires more energy and this is subtracted from the model's momentum. The result is that although an increase of aerodynamic lift was produced at first, as the airspeed falls, the lift force becomes smaller again (Figure 2.17). At the lower speed, a higher angle of attack is required to sustain the model. The elevator will probably have to be raised again to achieve the steady climb (Phase 3).

The wing lift in a climb is somewhat less than the weight, since the

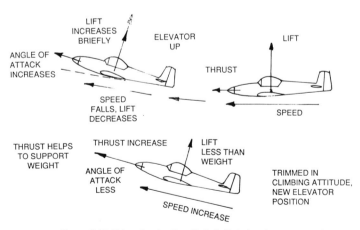

Figure 2.17 Trimming for the climb. Initial elevator movement increases angle of attack, model starts to climb. Speed is reduced, so aerodynamic forces also reduced. To maintain speed, power increase requires new elevator trim.

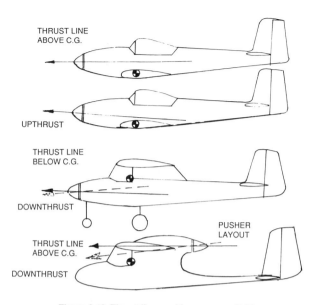

THRUST LINE
ABOVE C.G.

UPTHRUST

THRUST LINE
BELOW C.G.

DOWNTHRUST

THRUST LINE
ABOVE C.G.

DOWNTHRUST

PUSHER
LAYOUT

Figure 2.18 Thrust line position causes pitching
moments about the centre of gravity. These are
normally balanced out by appropriate elevator
position. Variations of power cause changes of
the moments. Adjustments of the thrust line
(downthrust and upthrust) minimise or increase
these effects, but changes of airspeed caused
by power variations are more important.

tilting of the thrust axis transfers some of the supporting force to the propeller, but with small climbing angles this is not very important.

The effects of thrust line position on trim have been mentioned already (2.2 above). Variations in power cause changes in the pitching moments as suggested in Figure 2.17. A much more important effect arises because power changes alter the airspeed and, as stressed several times before, all aerodynamic forces are greatly affected by flow speeds.

Suppose that with the model climbing at a slow airspeed, the pilot opens the engine throttle enough to bring the speed in the climb back to what it was in level flight. Moving the throttle is Phase 1 of a new control action, and Phase 2 checks the throttle at a new flight velocity, up the inclined path. The increased airspeed creates more wing lift than is needed to support the model and the extra thrust will take more share of the supporting load too. The excess of upward force will cause the model to tilt to a steeper angle of climb. With a very large power increase this nose up pitching caused by the extra upward forces may carry the model into a loop. The pilot does not intend to loop but wishes only to keep climbing at a steady angle with more power. In Phase 3 the trim therefore has to be changed to a more *nose down* balance, to *reduce* the angle of attack. Compared with the slow climb, which required fairly generous up elevator trim, the fast climb at the same angle requires less up, or even slightly down, elevator. Where the elevator actually has to be held for a given angle of climb will depend on the airspeed and the throttle setting. The final elevator position will be different from the movement needed at first to initiate the climb. To maintain the climb at a certain angle and rate of ascent, the final position of the controls, once the climb is under way, may be up elevator, or elevator neutral, or even down elevator, depending on the airspeed and power used. The elevator is used to control the angle of attack to produce the amount of lift necessary for whatever flight position the pilot requires. The actual control positions required to hold a trim are sometimes quite surprising and vary from one model to the next.

In aerobatics, the controls are constantly changing but it remains true that each attitude taken up in flight requires a trim setting different from that required to get the model into that position.

In summary, it may be useful to run through a few simple man-oeuvres showing how these principles of control and trim operate in practice.

2.6 Taking off

When a model is to take off, it must move forward through the air at a speed and angle of attack sufficient to create enough lift at least to equal the weight. Since it is the air speed, not the ground speed, that determines this, the take off is best made into wind, since the airflow over the wings will already be appreciable before the model moves. The result is a shorter take off run and the aerodynamic controls also begin to work effectively at once. Taking off downwind is hazardous since in the early stages the airflow over all surfaces (except perhaps those within the slipstream) is in the wrong direction and the controls do not work. Even if the early ground run is managed, the model must roll for a long way, at high ground speed, before it can reach flying airspeed. The space required for take off will be excessive.

Normally, full engine power will be used to accelerate the model quickly. Aerodynamic drag as well as wheel drag resists the thrust. To reduce aerodynamic drag, in the early stages the elevator is used to trim the model at a low drag angle of attack, which means it is brought as close as possible to its best L/D angle while still on the ground. (Tricycle undercarriages are best arranged to approximate this ground attitude, but 'tail dragging' aeroplanes need to get their tail up as soon as there is sufficient airspeed to allow the elevator to work.)

During the ground run, the rudder is used to counteract any tendency for the model to yaw either to left or right. Such swinging forces arise from the slipstream effect on the vertical stabilisers, from the torque of the propeller, and, with tail dragging aeroplanes, from the gyroscopic reaction as the tail comes up (see 6.11). It is useless to try to increase the angle of attack to take off before flying speed is reached. This can only increase the drag and will actually slow the model down. When flying speed is reached, the angle of attack is increased by the elevator and the model leaves the ground. Normally, with full power, a climb will be established at once. The trimming requirements for this have been discussed in outline above. The elevator control stick will normally have to be moved forward slightly to prevent the model rearing up steeply at full throttle.

2.7 Flying straight and level

In straight and level flight a balance is established so that the total lift, including any contribution from stabiliser and other components than the wing, is exactly equal to the weight. Since the lift force depends, like all aerodynamic reactions, on flight speed, the angle of attack required for lift to equal weight will vary according to the flight speed. That in turn depends on the thrust and drag. At slow speed, the required lift will be obtained only if the angle of attack is high, which normally requires some nose up attitude. At high speed, a lower angle of attack is required so the attitude is nose down. With a typical sports flying model the elevator will not be in its neutral position in fast flight, but will be down. In slow flight, it will be up. At one speed only the elevator will be neutral. This should be close to the trim for least drag or best L/D. If the rigging angles of incidence are wrong, the pilot will observe that the fuselage is not aligned with the flight direction when the elevator is in neutral. This creates extra drag. Its importance for ordinary sport flying should not be exaggerated.

With a racing aircraft, minimising fuselage and stabiliser drag at high speed is very important, so the fuselage should be aligned with the flight direction with elevator neutral at full power. Whether it is so or not will depend mainly on the care taken by the designer to get the angles of incidence right during the design stages. Such a model will then appear distinctly 'nose up' at all other flight speeds.

2.8 Turning

As mentioned above, to turn the model, it must be banked, the angle of bank determining the rate of turn (Figure 2.3). The ailerons are used for this, or, if the model has only rudder and elevator controls, the wing is banked by yawing the model, compelling the dihedral to bank the wing. No bank, no turn. A proportion of the wing lift force is directed sideways, how much depending on the angle of bank. Since a proportion of the lift is directed horizontally, it is immediately obvious to the pilot that there is insufficient support. To increase the total wing lift force so that it can both turn the model and support it vertically, the elevator is used to increase the angle of attack. More engine power may also be needed, since the increase of lift increases the wing drag and tends to slow the model down.

With a glider, a steep turn necessarily increases the rate of sink. However, attempting to turn a sailplane without adequate bank causes serious skidding, so bringing the model down even more rapidly than a correctly banked turn.

If the angle of attack is increased too much in a turn the wing will stall, so caution must be used. Turning without adequate bank is a common cause of stalling and, because of the difference in angles of attack of the two wings, the inner wing tends to stall first. This often leads to a spin (see 2.13 below).

Application of ailerons always causes some adverse yaw, as described above, and this may be countered with the rudder. In powered models, this effect is often not very apparent and requires little attention, except sometimes at low flying speeds on low power, as when coming in to land. With sailplanes, co-ordination of rudder with ailerons is almost always essential if the turn is to be efficiently performed, and it is common practice to couple these two controls.

Once in the turn, often the ailerons and rudder can be returned to neutral or nearly so, perhaps with a little 'hold off' bank. The elevator, however, must remain trimmed up slightly to maintain the turning and supporting force from the wing.

To come out of a turn, the model is rolled to bring the bank to zero. Since all the lift force is then directed upwards, if height is to be kept the same, the elevator will need to be re-trimmed for a lower angle of attack.

2.9 Landing

To land, the engine is normally throttled back and the model becomes, in effect, a glider. The objective is to place the model accurately at the desired touch down point, facing into wind, and stall the wing just as the wheels meet the ground, so that the aircraft will not bounce into the air again. To achieve this perfectly every time is not easy. It is better to touch down a little too fast, even if it means a slight bounce, than to stall the model when it is still some distance above the ground but with insufficient height for recovery.

The most likely places for serious mistakes in landing are during the approach, when turns have to be made with low power and high angles of attack. The elevator should be used cautiously, and if there is any doubt in the pilot's mind, the model's nose should be lowered. When the model is aligned into wind and pointing at the landing spot, the angle of attack must still be controlled and the temptation to level out too soon, with up elevator movement, must be resisted. Apart from the danger of stalling, gusts of wind causing the model to bank or yaw cannot be counteracted promptly if the flow speed over the ailerons and rudder (with little slipstream effect) is too slow. Assuming the model has been steered to the right place and is just above the ground, a gradual easing of the elevator should produce a gentle stall or a touch down with only minimal excess speed. Once on the ground, the rudder is used to keep straight.

In taxying after landing, it is often necessary to increase engine power to blow some slipstream over the rudder, unless a steerable tail or nosewheel is fitted, and even then the resistance of the wheels to rolling on rough ground may necessitate some extra thrust.

2.10 Looping

If the pilot wishes the model to loop the loop, starting from level flight, enough thrust must be provided to keep the airspeed up as the model climbs and rotates through the vertical position and over. Speed will be regained as the model comes out of the inverted position in the second half of the loop. Elevator and throttle should, ideally, be controlled throughout to produce a perfectly circular path. At the extreme uppermost point of the loop, the forces on the wing should be still in the normal direction. That is, the wing will be resisting an upward inertia force by 'lifting' downwards. An imaginary pilot in the cockpit should not 'hang in the straps'. In a full-sized aircraft performing a good loop, dust on the floor of the cockpit remains there throughout.

If the flight velocity through the air is not sufficient, the model will not be able to complete the first quarter of the loop and will reach its stalling speed and fall away. In a badly executed loop the model may hang at the half inverted position, lose flying speed, stall inverted and flop over. With a low powered model or a glider, loops may be done by diving initially to gain the necessary airspeed to carry the model over.

To perform an inverted loop requires similar considerations of speed in relation to lift. As the model noses over or 'bunts' from level flight, gravity helps it to accelerate and there is no difficulty then in diving through into the inverted position. The flight speed at the bottom of the loop may be sufficient to carry the model through the early part of the recovery but very possibly, before reaching the vertical attitude again, ascending, the speed will fall off and a stall will result. Manoeuvres in pitch, therefore, always require good judgement of flying speed and, often, co-ordinated use of the power control to maintain adequate flow speeds over the wing.

2.11 Rolling

There are basically three types of roll. The simplest to perform is the barrel roll, which is in effect a loop drawn out laterally into a helix. As with a loop, loads on the structure are normal and dust on the cockpit floor should be undisturbed. The angle of attack must be increased to provide excess lift, and as the model begins to climb, the ailerons are used to bank over. The rudder may be needed to prevent yawing. As the model nears the vertically banked position the elevator must still be used to maintain a positive angle of attack while the ailerons keep the roll going. The aeroplane then continues to climb and reaches the wings level position with the elevators still up and the wing lift therefore downwards relative to the ground. The second half of the roll is a continuation with elevator still up and the ailerons still continuing the roll, to recover ideally at the same height as the start.

The slow or axial roll does involve reversed loading. In full-sized flying, dust should be cleaned out of the cockpit before doing such a manoeuvre, since it may get in the pilot's eyes at a crucial moment! Also, at two critical points, when the wing is vertical, the fuselage and engine thrust are called upon to provide the support which the wing can no longer give. With full engine power, the elevator is used to increase the angle of attack slightly and the ailerons initiate a roll around the longitudinal (X) axis, the rudder being used to keep the model straight. As the wings approach the vertical, the elevator must progressively reduce the angle of attack to zero (aerodynamically) since any lift when the wings are banked will initiate a turn. The rudder is used progressively to tilt the thrust line upwards so that the power of the engine can support the weight, together with some lift contribution obtained by tilting the fuselage (Figure 2.10).

The roll is then continued to the inverted position, which requires the wing to be at a negative angle of attack relative to the aeroplane's axes, but positive in relation to the ground. The elevator is therefore moved progressively down relative to the model (up relative to the ground). The ailerons are still fully applied to keep the roll going. The second half of the roll requires the same kind of control movements as the first half, but in the opposite sense, so that at the vertical point the rudder tilts the fuselage up to give support as the wings pass through zero again. Co-ordination of the slow roll is not easy.

The third type of roll, the flick roll, is really a form of spinning with the axis of the spin horizontal (see 2.13, below).

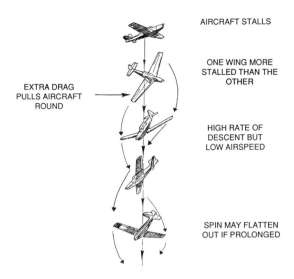

AIRCRAFT STALLS

ONE WING MORE
STALLED THAN THE
OTHER

EXTRA DRAG
PULLS AIRCRAFT
ROUND

HIGH RATE OF
DESCENT BUT
LOW AIRSPEED

SPIN MAY FLATTEN
OUT IF PROLONGED

Figure 2.19 Spinning

2.12 Flying inverted

Inverted flight is basically the same as flying upright, although it feels different to the pilot. The wing must be maintained at an angle of attack that yields lift, and this requires elevator trim such that the wing is at a negative angle of attack relative to the normal control planes. In this attitude, depending on the shape of the wing in cross section and its rigging angle of incidence, the aeroplane may appear to be flying at an abnormally nose high attitude. Once this attitude is accepted, the controls continue to work as when upright, but because the loads are reversed, they produce reversed effects from the point of view of the radio control pilot on the ground. Practice is required before the model flier becomes confident. The feeling is quite different from that of the pilot in a full-sized aeroplane who is inverted with the aircraft.

Once familiarity has been gained with this, all manoeuvres that are possible from the upright starting position can be attempted from the inverted situation and all the same problems arise.

2.13 Spinning

Spinning, sometimes called 'autorotation', is a condition in which the whole mainplane of the aircraft is stalled, but one side is at a higher angle of attack than the other (Figure 2.19). Although the stall extends right across from tip to tip, one wing is more deeply stalled than the other, so there is less lift and more drag on this side. The model loses height rapidly and rotates, nose down, as the extra drag pulls the lower wing back. The aeroplane is in a constantly yawed condition; in a right handed spin with the right wing low and more stalled than the left, the aircraft is constantly skidding to the left. The vertical stabiliser, if in the usual place at the tail end, meets the airflow from the left. Meanwhile, since the lift is less on the right side, the aircraft is rolling to the right. This spinning descent will continue until the wing is unstalled.

An ordinary stall can usually be converted into a spin if, at the moment of flow separation, the aeroplane is yawed sharply by use of the rudder. This not only starts the rotation but ensures that the wing on the inner side of the spin will stall first and thereafter be at a greater angle of attack than the other. It is because a wing that stalls at the tips first tends to drop a wing in the stall and enter an unintended spin that such tip stalling tendencies are dangerous.

To recover from a spin, it is necessary to restore the angle of attack of the wing to within its normal operating range. Sometimes recovery occurs immediately down elevator is applied, but it is frequently found in practice that the elevator will not bring the aircraft out of the stall until the rotation in the spin has been stopped or slowed down. This requires the use of the rudder against the spin, prior to or simultaneously with the elevator. Hence, to recover from a right handed spin, the standard procedure is to apply full opposite rudder, to the left, and then move the elevator progressively to pitch the nose down and restore the unstalled condition. Since the aircraft in a spin is already nose down the inexperienced pilot may be reluctant to pitch the aircraft into an even steeper attitude, but this must be done. When the spin has been arrested in this way, the model will emerge in a steep dive and will pick up speed rapidly. Once the angle of attack has been reduced, a normal dive recovery can be carried out. There is always a considerable loss of height, both during the spin and in the diving recovery. It is important that if spinning is to be done deliberately, it should be at a good height.

Unintentional spinning can be prevented by avoiding excessively high angles of attack which stall the wing. The primary control involved in preventing spins is therefore the elevator.

The ailerons are usually of little use in preventing a spin and may in fact encourage one to begin, if used coarsely. The natural tendency on finding one wing going down is to apply aileron to restore level flight. If the aeroplane is on the point of stalling this may be quite the wrong thing to do, since lowering the aileron on the downgoing side is in effect to increase the angle of attack still further and to increase drag on that side too, so yawing the aircraft and precipitating the asymmetrical stall. If a spin seems likely, the rudder should be used to prevent yawing while the elevator restores a safe angle of attack. After this, aileron function becomes normal again.

When in a spin, ailerons may sometimes assist recovery if used in conjunction with the rudder to stop the rotation, but this does not always mean they need to be applied with the rudder to the same side. Each aircraft is different in this respect and in most cases the ailerons are best left in the central, neutral, position during spin recovery.

In a spin, the angle of yaw can be very large and the vertical surfaces of fin and rudder may be at such an angle of attack that they verge on the stall. If this happens, the rudder may be incapable of providing the necessary side force to stop the spin and recovery may be impossible. For this reason, even though very large vertical stabilising surfaces are not necessary for most ordinary flight attitudes, they often prove to be required for spin recovery. In the development of full-sized aircraft, many prototypes have required modification to the vertical tail areas after the preliminary spinning trials. Fin strakes and dorsal extensions have frequently been added. In some instances, the tailplane has been found to 'blanket' the fin, disrupting the airflow in the spin and necessitating a repositioning or even a complete redesign of the tail unit. It is also to be expected that slipstream effects on the vertical stabiliser will make a difference to the spin recovery. In some instances, an aeroplane which will not recover from a spin with the engine throttled back may be saved by opening the throttle and thus increasing the flow speed over the rudder and increasing its effect.

A particularly dangerous form of spin is the flat spin. In this, the rate of rotation becomes so rapid that centrifugal forces on the front and rear fuselage and outer wing panels increase rapidly and tend to flatten out the attitude of the aircraft until it resembles a spinning boomerang. In this condition, the vertical stabiliser is completely stalled since the airflow meets it at a very high angle. The wing and horizontal stabilisers are also deeply stalled and recovery may be impossible. Fortunately, providing the aeroplane has its centre of gravity fairly well ahead of the aerodynamic centre, the true, irrecoverable flat spin is a rarity.

If a model is flying straight and level, but is pulled sharply to a high angle of attack position, a high speed stall will result. If at this moment, the rudder is used to yaw the aircraft, what happens is a spin around a horizontal axis, or flick roll. If allowed to do so, the flick will develop into a descending spin, but if recovery (rudder against the roll, down elevator) is initiated at the right moment, the model emerges, unstalled, flying straight and level again. Variations of this manoeuvre include upward and downward flick rolls, spins around climbing or descending axes, and inverted flick rolls which are exactly the same in principle but involve stalling the wing in its inverted sense.

The spin should not be confused with the spiral dive. A spiral dive is a descending turn with steep bank and a steep diving angle. The airspeed rises rapidly but the wing is not stalled and recovery is straightforward. The main danger, apart from hitting the ground, is that the high loads involved in the very fast turning dive, or a sharp pulling out recovery, may break the wings. In a spin, because the drag of the stalled wing is so high, the airspeed is relatively low.

3 WING SECTIONS

3.1 Wing lift

A wing, or other wing-like surface such as a stabiliser, converts most of the aerodynamic reaction on it into a useful lift force at right angles to the flight direction. It is only necessary to experiment briefly with a piece of card, or a flat piece of balsa or plywood, to show that a thin sheet of stiff material, held at a moderate angle of attack to the flow of air, produces lift (Figure 3.1). The effect arises in all cases because there is a difference in air pressure between the upper and lower surfaces. It is the *total pressure difference* which creates the force. A reduction of pressure on the upper surface will generate lift even if the pressure under the wing is not higher than the normal or *static pressure* of the undisturbed air. This is often misunderstood. High and low pressure are relative terms. Often, because of the detailed shape of the wing *profile* (cross section or *aerofoil section*) the pressure on the underside of the wing is actually lower than the static pressure, on average, although this is called the high pressure side. Depending on the angle of attack, so long as the average pressure on the upper side is lower than that below the wing, lift results.

3.2 Wing drag

The drag of a wing is composed of three parts (Figure 3.2). The *form drag* or *pressure drag* is caused by the general disturbance of the air

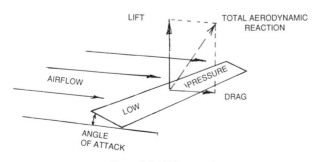

Figure 3.1 Lift from a wing

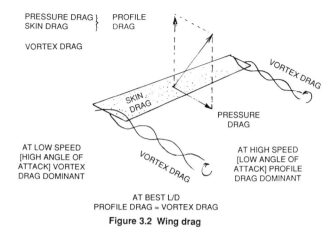

PRESSURE DRAG }
SKIN DRAG } PROFILE DRAG

VORTEX DRAG

SKIN DRAG

VORTEX DRAG

PRESSURE DRAG

AT LOW SPEED
[HIGH ANGLE OF
ATTACK] VORTEX
DRAG DOMINANT

VORTEX DRAG

AT HIGH SPEED
[LOW ANGLE OF
ATTACK] PROFILE
DRAG DOMINANT

AT BEST L/D
PROFILE DRAG = VORTEX DRAG

Figure 3.2 Wing drag

and the pressure differences which arise. The *skin drag* is caused by friction and slight stickiness or viscosity of the air in close contact with the skin of the wing. The *vortex* or *induced drag* is caused by the formation of rotating vortices where the air tends to flow crosswise relative to the general stream. (It is possible to divide the drag of any object in streamlined flow into these three components.) Taken together, form and skin drag are often termed *profile drag,* which is the drag force measured in the wind tunnel when a wing is under test. Vortex drag is not usually measured in the wind tunnel, but depends on the planform of the wing, as explained in Chapter 4.

3.3 The pitching moment of wings
Like most other objects in fluid flow, wings often develop pitching moments tending to change their angle of attack. While the average pressure over upper and lower surfaces is responsible for the lift, pressure variations from place to place above and below cause the pitching moment to arise. How powerful this force on a wing is at a given speed depends chiefly on the camber (see 3.10 below). In the case of wings with symmetrical profile, the pitching moment is zero at normal angles of attack. With normal cambered profiles, the pitching moment is negative or nose down. This *negative pitching moment* is normally resisted by the stabiliser, which has to be set at such an angle of attack to the air that it produces the required balancing force at all times (see Figure 1.5).

At the stall the negative pitching moment increases sharply. This is why models normally pitch nose down when stalling.

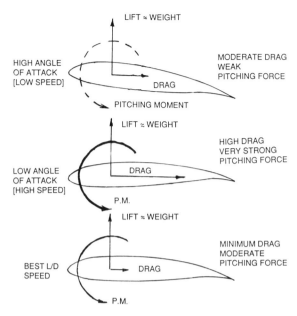

Figure 3.3 The aerodynamic centre of
a wing [Eppler 861-3-914 profile]

3.4 The aerodynamic centre of a wing

As with any object in streamlined flow, a wing has an aerodynamic
centre. The three basic aerodynamic forces, lift, drag and pitching
moment, act here. At angles of attack less than the stalling angle, the
aerodynamic centre does not move. At each cross sectional point on
the wing, the local aerodynamic centre is always very close to the
quarter chord or 25% position and, in the vertical sense, near the
camber or mean line, midway between upper and lower surfaces of
the aerofoil (Figure 3.3). If the wing is not swept back or forward, the
aerodynamic centre is thus at the 25% position at the root of the wing,
but with swept wings allowance must be made for the sweep. The
aerodynamic centre of a complete wing is at the 25% position of the
mean aerodynamic chord of the wing, viewed in plan. This is discussed again briefly in the next chapter.

3.5 The centre of pressure

Another way of describing the forces on a wing is to attribute the pitching force to the movements of an abstract theoretical point, called the
centre of pressure. This is imagined as moving backwards when the
angle of attack decreases and forwards again as the angle increases,
up to the stall, when it moves aft again. The nose down pitching tend-

ency of all cambered wings can be explained as due to the action of the lift at the centre of pressure acting on a variable lever or moment arm (Figure 3.4). In early wind tunnel work, the three basic forces actually felt and measured on the wing were reduced to two, lift and drag, and a calculation was then done to work out the supposed location of the centre of pressure. The calculated positions were charted as centre of pressure movements, expressed in terms of percentages of the wing chord. This method of explaining the pitching moment led to various difficulties. The chief of these was that, at low angles of attack, the calculations showed the centre of pressure as lying at more than 100% of the chord, that is, behind the trailing edge. In very high speed flight, the centre of pressure has to be imagined even beyond the tail of the aircraft. To suppose that the lift produced by a wing acts at some distance behind the wing altogether is rather difficult. In a vertical dive the wing lift is zero. The calculation shows the centre of pressure at an infinite distance behind the aircraft, which is equivalent to its being imagined out of the universe! The pitching moment, however, is a very real force, not imaginary. It does not disappear, but increases as the aeroplane dives more steeply. This is the prime cause of some un-

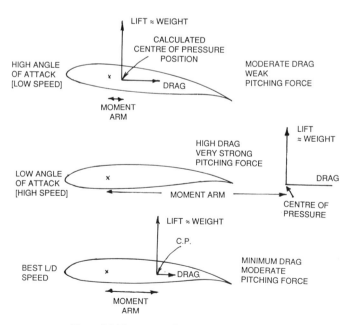

Figure 3.4 The centre of pressure theory used to explain the nose down pitching moment of cambered wings

stable or marginally stable aircraft 'tucking under' into the inverted position from fast flight.

The three forces actually felt by a wing and measured in the wind tunnel all act at, or close to, the 25% mean chord point, and although the centre of pressure theory is mathematically correct, it is best replaced by the aerodynamic centre concept, which describes exactly the same facts in a more practical way.

3.6 Air pressure and flow velocity

The pressure changes over and under a wing arise because there is a close connection between air pressure and flow speed. The energy contained in a flow of air is constant. It may be thought of as being of two kinds, pressure and momentum, which may interchange, pressure becoming speed, or speed becoming pressure, while the total energy remains the same. When the speed of flow over a wing increases, energy is subtracted from the pressure and converted to momentum. The greater the acceleration of the flow, the more energy is converted, reducing the pressure. Conversely, if the flow is slowed down, some of the energy of motion it contains will be changed back to pressure energy. Wherever the flow is forced to speed up, the pressure falls. When the flow slows down, the opposite occurs, momentum energy is re-converted and the pressure rises.

When air flows around a wing, or any other obstruction, since it is a fluid substance it cannot pile up anywhere as snow or blowing sand might do. Exactly as much air must leave the neighbourhood of the wing in each unit of time as arrives (Figure 3.5). Since the flow has to

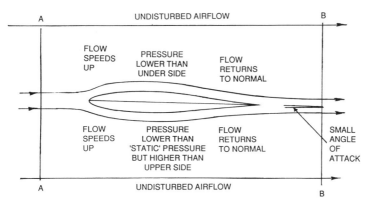

Figure 3.5 As much air flows past B-B in each moment as arrives at A-A. To pass round the wing the flow must accelerate. Pressure falls where flow speed rises. Lift results only if pressure above the wing is lower on average than below

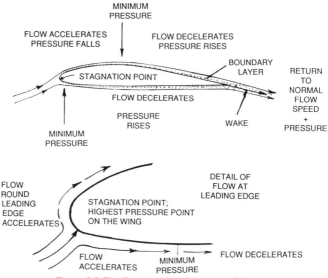

Figure 3.6 The flow round a wing at a positive (lifting) angle of attack

pass round the wing the route it follows is longer than if there was no obstruction. The flow must speed up in order to reach the trailing edge together with the rest of the flow. Any other possibility would lead to air somewhere accumulating in a heap, which cannot occur in the normal atmosphere.

The way in which pressure alters around a wing in flight, to give lift and pressure drag, is thus determined by the change of flow speed at each point. At a suitable angle of attack, the air meets the wing at a point called the *stagnation point,* slightly below the extreme leading edge, and divides from there to pass either below or above the wing (Figure 3.6). The air going over the upper side actually has to flow slightly forwards at first to pass round the leading edge. To do so it speeds up rapidly, causing a pressure fall over the forward part of the wing. At some point, depending on the exact contour of the aerofoil section, this upper side flow will reach a maximum velocity which coincides with the minimum pressure. After passing this place, the upper surface air will slow down gradually, the pressure rising again, until at the trailing edge both flow speed and pressure are practically back to normal. On the underside, the same kind of thing happens. The flow speeds up and slows down again after passing the minimum pressure point. There is often a *reduction* of pressure below the wing just as there is above, but if the angle of attack of the wing is set for lift, the *average* pressure over the whole lower surface is more than that

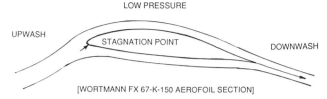

LOW PRESSURE

UPWASH

STAGNATION POINT

DOWNWASH

[WORTMANN FX 67-K-150 AEROFOIL SECTION]

Figure 3.7 Upwash and downwash of a lifting wing

above. Providing the general flow pattern remains streamlined, the relation of pressure to speed is quite exact.

A small amount of air on both surfaces of the wing will tend to be
dragged along because of skin drag, forming a thin, slower moving
layer called the *boundary layer.* The two boundary layers, upper and
lower, combine at the trailing edge to form a wake of disturbed air
which trails behind the wing. (This wake can strike any other surfaces
behind the mainplane, reducing their efficiency.)

The reduced average pressure over the upper surface of a lifting
wing is felt, at subsonic flight speeds, some distance ahead of the
wing itself (Figure 3.7). This causes the airflow to start moving upwards, towards the low pressure side, before the leading edge is
reached. The streamlines bend upwards ahead of the wing, so the
angle at which the flow finally meets the leading edge is not the same
as the angle of attack of the wing to the flight direction. This upward
turning of the flow is called *upwash.* Behind the wing there is a corresponding equal *downwash.* (These upwash and downwash effects are
only part of the story. In flight, there is an additional very powerful
downwash effect created by *wing tip vortices.* These will be discussed
in the next chapter.)

3.7 Flat plate wings

Simple flat plates are quite efficient lifting surfaces at low angles of
attack. Because they are so thin, they disturb the air little as it passes
over and under them, so they are quite capable of producing lift with
small drag forces, mostly skin friction. Such shapes are very suitable
for the stabilisers and fins of radio controlled model aeroplanes which
are not, or should not be, expected to support large lift loads. They
operate only within two or three degrees on either side of the zero
angle of attack. For very small models, such as 'toy' gliders and
aeroplanes, the flat plate wing has the advantage of being easily
made and repaired.

For larger models flat plate wings have structural and aerodynamic
defects. They lack stiffness, bending and twisting too easily when

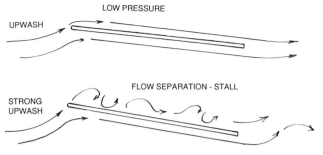

Figure 3.8 Flat plate wings at low and high angles
of attack

loads increase. Also, at angles of attack more than a few degrees
either side of zero, the airflow tends to separate sharply from the leading edge of the wing, i.e., the flat plate wing profile stalls too early
(Figure 3.8).

3.8 Curved plate wings

Some improvement in both lifting ability and strength can be achieved
by using slightly curved or *cambered* plate sections. Arching a sheet
of card or thin wood increases stiffness greatly. At positive angles of
attack where a flat plate would stall, the curvature of the camber leads
the airflow smoothly over the wing, instead of confronting the flow with
a very abrupt change of direction. The angle of attack at which the
flow meets the wing most smoothly, tangential to the curvature, is in-
fluenced considerably by the upwash. As the angle of attack increases, the strength of the upwash also increases, so the flow to
some extent adjusts itself to the curve of the wing before actually passing the leading edge (Figure 3.9). For very light and slow flying model
aircraft such curved plates are the most efficient wing profiles.

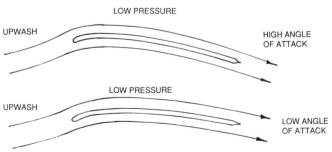

Figure 3.9 Curved plate wings

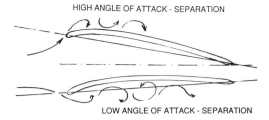

HIGH ANGLE OF ATTACK - SEPARATION

LOW ANGLE OF ATTACK - SEPARATION

Figure 3.10 The useful angle of attack range
of thin curved plate wings is small

It is still the case that at angles of attack a few degrees higher or lower than that at which the air meets the leading edge most naturally (allowing for the upwash effect), the flow has to change direction suddenly and separation may result. For a curved plate, therefore, there is a rather narrow range of angles of attack over which the wing will work effectively and if it is at an angle outside this range the flow will not follow the contour of the wing (Figure 3.10). At high angles the flow separates from the upper surface and at low angles from the lower surface. Controlling models with thin wings is not easy, requiring care at all times to keep the angle of attack within narrow limits.

3.9 Thick wing sections

For all aeroplanes above a certain size and weight, the thin plate wing, whether cambered or not, is not strong enough to withstand the air loads placed upon it in flight. The wing must be made thick enough to allow internal structure, such as spars or supporting plastic foam, to distribute and carry the stresses. Simple bending up and down is the most obvious kind of stress on a wing, but twisting forces, caused chiefly by the pitching moments, are equally important. While the curved plate is quite resistant to bending, it has very poor resistance in twisting or *torsion*.

Thick wing sections also have very important aerodynamic advantages. If the leading edge of the wing is smoothly rounded instead of

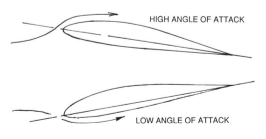

HIGH ANGLE OF ATTACK

LOW ANGLE OF ATTACK

Figure 3.11 The wide useful range of angles
of attack of thick aerofoil sections

being more or less sharp, the air is never forced to change direction abruptly. There is much less danger of flow separation and the result is that a thick wing can operate efficiently over a wider range of angles of attack than a thin plate (Figure 3.11). Up to a point, this widening of the useful range of angles becomes greater as the wing becomes thicker.

Hence not only is thick wing stronger and stiffer than a thin one of similar weight, span and area, but it is also more tolerant of variations of speed and trim and is altogether more practical. At the rather exact angle of attack at which the thin plate gives its best results, it will usually still create less profile drag than a thicker wing, but at angles slightly greater or less, the thick wing has the advantage. Up to a point, the thicker a wing is, the wider its useful range of angles of attack and the easier it is to trim. More is said about this below (3.16).

Wing thicknesses are measured in terms of percentages of the wing chord. Hence a wing which is 5 units thick with a chord of 50 units would be 10% thick, one with a chord of 100 units and thickness of 5 units would be 5% thick and so on. In full sized aviation, wing thicknesses may vary from two or three up to twenty or even more percent. Models generally fly with wings between 5 and 15% thick, although some scale models with profiles up to 21% have flown successfully and a flat plate section may be only 1 or 2% of the chord in thickness.

3.10 Camber

Inside every fat person, it has been said, is a thin one trying to get out. This might be applied to wing sections. One of the most important features of any wing section is its camber, which is the curvature of the *centre line, mean line* or *skeleton* of the profile (Figure 3.12). The mean line is the line which follows a path equal in distance from the

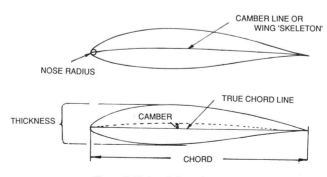

Figure 3.12 Aerofoil section geometry

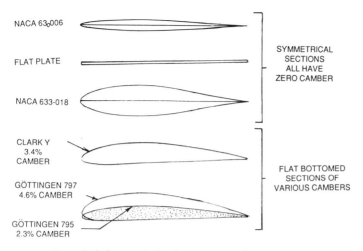

Figure 3.13 Symmetrical and cambered aerofoil sections

upper and lower surfaces of the profile. Any wing section whatever can therefore be imagined as containing a very thin plate or skeleton wing profile. Just as the skeleton of a human being determines many important physical features of the person, the hidden camber line of a wing profile determines many of its vital characteristics. In particular, the camber of a profile determines its best angle of attack and its pitching moment, one of the most important forces which has to be balanced out when trimming an aeroplane (See 3.3). Camber also has a major effect on the stalling behaviour of the wing and on the profile drag.

It is very common among model fliers and writers of books and articles about wing sections for models to classify wing profiles by their outward appearance only, ignoring the vitally important skeleton. Terms like 'flat bottomed', 'undercambered', 'semi symmetrical' and 'Phillips entry' are used freely. (The last term seems to have originated with Horatio Phillips, the pioneer research worker of about 100 years ago.) These expressions are so entrenched that it may be impossible now to eliminate them, but for the sake of clarity and simplicity, they should probably be abandoned. A wing section is either fully symmetrical or it is cambered. The amount and type of camber varies considerably from one so-called 'flat bottomed' or 'semi symmetrical' profile to another. These variations make a great difference in practical flying and much confusion results if sections which are really very different are classified together under one term.

A *symmetrical* aerofoil section has *zero camber*, the line midway between upper and lower surfaces is perfectly straight (Figure 3.13).

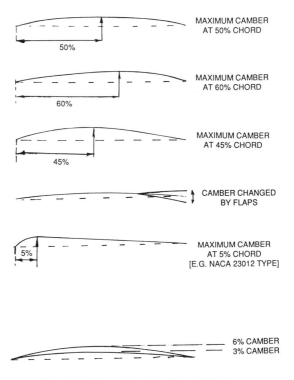

MAXIMUM CAMBER
AT 50% CHORD

50%

MAXIMUM CAMBER
AT 60% CHORD

60%

MAXIMUM CAMBER
AT 45% CHORD

45%

CAMBER CHANGED
BY FLAPS

MAXIMUM CAMBER
AT 5% CHORD
[E.G. NACA 23012 TYPE]

5%

6% CAMBER
3% CAMBER

**Figure 3.14 Types of camber. Every thick wing
section is built around a 'skeleton' or mean line**

The profile may be thick or thin, it may have its point of greatest thickness fairly near the leading edge or further aft, but if it is symmetrical the camber line will be straight. It will therefore share some of its most important aerodynamic characteristics with all other symmetrical wing sections. All such symmetrical sections behave to some extent like flat plates in that, at zero angle of attack, they generate zero lift. At positive angles of attack a symmetrical section will produce lift. The profile drag created by a symmetrical section will be least at zero angle of attack and zero lift. How much the drag increases as the angle of attack is moved from zero depends on the detail of the outer symmetrical form. The principles outlined above apply. A thick symmetrical wing is capable of operating successfully, giving lift with only moderate drag, over a wide range of angles of attack on either side of zero. A thin symmetrical wing is efficient but only over a narrow range.

Symmetrical wings, providing there is no flow separation, have zero pitching moment at all usable angles of attack.

If the camber line is not straight, the section is cambered to some extent. Putting this the other way round, if the external shape is not *perfectly* symmetrical, the section is cambered, and much depends then on just what the camber is. This cannot be determined merely by making a casual external examination. This is where terms like 'semi symmetrical' and 'Phillips entry' are most misleading. What has to be discovered is the exact shape of the 'thin wing' trying to get out of the thick one.

The amount of camber is measured in percentage terms, relative to the chord line of the aerofoil (Figure 3.14). On an outline of the profile, a straight line is first drawn from the extreme leading edge of the aerofoil to the trailing edge. This is the *true chord line*. (Any line not passing through both leading edge and trailing edge is not the true chord line.) The mean line is then a curved line joining the same two extreme points. The *maximum camber* is the greatest distance of the mean line from the chord line and this is expressed as a percentage of the chord. Useful aerofoils in practice have cambers of less than 10%. Commonly, slow flying free flight model aircraft use cambers of 6 and 7%. Radio controlled sport flying models may have camber of up to 5% though this is rather high. Values around 2 and 3% are more usual and, of course, aerobatic models usually have symmetrical profiles in which the camber line and the true chord line coincide.

The camber line may be curved in various ways, each change having some effect on the way the model behaves in flight.

By calculation, it has been possible to discover a camber line which distributes the load equally over the chord from front to rear. This makes for efficiency, since every part of the wing, all of which produces profile drag, also contributes its full share of lift. The stall also is

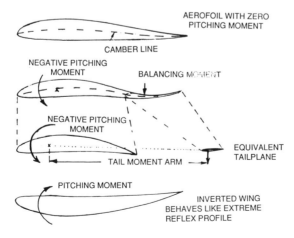

Figure 3.15 Reflex camber

gradual, beginning, usually, at the trailing edge and moving forward rather than the flow separating abruptly from the leading edge. Unless there is some pressing need for a different type of camber, this constant type of loading distribution is generally the best (see table).

A special form of camber line, of reflex shape, attempts to get the best of both worlds (Figure 3.15). A symmetrical profile produces zero pitching moment, but is not very efficient at high angles of attack. The *reflex camber* form is carefully calculated to produce zero moment, but gains some advantage at positive angles of attack by being cambered over the forward part of the wing. This camber is then balanced out by reversed camber over the rear. In an ordinary model aeroplane with a tailplane, the pitching moment caused by the camber of the wing is balanced by the tailplane being trimmed to a negative angle of attack (see 1.5). The reflex type of profile, in a sense, carries its own tailplane, the negative rear part of the camber balancing the pitching moment of the front part. This unfortunately carries quite large drag penalties, so such reflex forms are used only where the pitching moment is a serious problem, as it may be with tailless or flying wing aircraft.

An extreme form of reflex camber may be used, which produces a nose-up pitching moment instead of the usual nose down force. There is rarely any advantage in this, and there is a considerable penalty to pay in terms of profile drag and stalling characteristics. It is interesting, all the same, that when a model with a normally cambered wing is flying inverted, the wing behaves like one with an extreme form of reflex camber. The natural tendency for an inverted, cambered wing is to raise the nose of the model. Relative to the model axes, there is no change in direction of the pitching moment which is still 'nose down' in this sense, but with the model itself upside down, nose down becomes nose up.

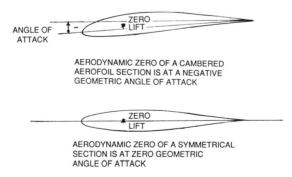

AERODYNAMIC ZERO OF A CAMBERED
AEROFOIL SECTION IS AT A NEGATIVE
GEOMETRIC ANGLE OF ATTACK

AERODYNAMIC ZERO OF A SYMMETRICAL
SECTION IS AT ZERO GEOMETRIC
ANGLE OF ATTACK

Figure 3.16 The aerodynamic zero

TABLE OF MEAN LINE ORDINATES
(Scale to required Camber by multiplication)

EVEN LOADING CAMBER		REFLEX FOR ZERO PITCHING MOMENT		CAMBER MAXIMUM AT 5% CHORD (NACA 210 SERIES)	
NACAA = 1.0 MEAN LINE				NACA 210 MEAN LINE	
CHORD STATION	ORDINATE	CHORD STATION	ORDINATE	CHORD STATION	ORDINATE
XU	YU	XU	YU		
0.000	0.000	0.000	0.000	XU	YU
.500	.250	5.000	3.240	0.000	0.000
.750	.350	10.000	5.770	1.250	.596
1.250	.535	15.000	7.650	2.500	.928
2.500	.930	20.000	8.940	5.000	1.114
5.000	1.580	25.000	9.700	7.500	1.087
7.500	2.120	30.000	9.990	10.000	1.058
10.000	2.585	35.000	9.880	15.000	.999
15.000	3.365	40.000	9.430	20.000	.940
20.000	3.980	45.000	8.700	25.000	.881
25.000	4.475	50.000	7.760	30.000	.823
30.000	4.860	55.000	6.660	40.000	.705
35.000	5.150	60.000	5.460	50.000	.588
40.000	5.355	65.000	4.240	60.000	.470
45.000	5.475	70.000	3.040	70.000	.353
50.000	5.515	75.000	1.940	80.000	.235
55.000	5.475	80.000	0.990	90.000	.118
60.000	5.355	85.000	0.260	95.000	.059
65.000	5.150	90.000	−0.190	100.000	0.000
70.000	4.860	95.000	−0.300		
75.000	4.475	100.000	0.000		
80.000	3.980				
85.000	3.365				
90.000	2.585				
95.000	1.580				
100.000	0.000				

METHOD

1. DRAW THE TRUE CHORD LINE, CORRECT LENGTH.
2. DIVIDE THE TRUE CHORD LINE INTO 100 UNITS AND MARK THE STATIONS GIVEN UNDER XU COLUMN IN THE TABLE
3. MULTIPLY THE FIGURES IN THE YU COLUMN TO GIVE THE DESIRED CAMBER MAXIMUM. (USE A CALCULATOR) E.G. 5.515 X 0.363 = 2% CAMBER, 4.475 X 0.363 = 1.62 AND SO ON. WRITE THE RESULTING ORDINATES IN A NEW COLUMN.
4. PLOT THE FINAL FIGURES AS VERTICAL OFFSETS ABOVE THE CHORD LINE AND JOIN WITH A SMOOTH CURVED LINE.

3.11 The influence of camber on lift

Commonly, model fliers speak of strongly cambered wing profiles as 'high lift' sections. It is true that a cambered wing at a given geometric angle of attack to the air will give more lift than a less cambered or symmetrical profile, but there is more to the matter than this. A symmetrical wing gives no lift when it is at zero angle of attack. A cambered wing can also be set at such a negative angle to the flow that it, too, gives no lift. At this negative angle, the cambered wing is at its *aerodynamic zero* (Figure 3.16). The symmetrical section is at aerodynamic zero when its geometrical angle to the flow is zero, but a cambered wing has an aerodynamic zero at some negative geometric angle. The more cambered the wing, the more negative the angle of aerodynamic zero is. If, now, angles of attack are measured from the aerodynamic zero in every case, symmetrical and cambered

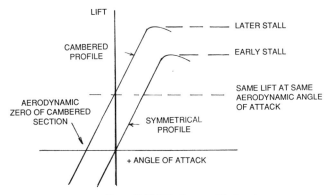

Figure 3.17 Lift of symmetrical and
cambered wings

wings give the same lift (Figure 3.17), over a range on either side of the aerodynamic zero angle.

The advantage of the cambered profile in terms of lift comes only when high angles of attack are considered. Measuring from the aerodynamic zero, when the symmetrical section is stalling, the cambered profile, because of the gentle leading in of the flow to the wing, is not stalled and continues to give useful lift. The stall comes later, aerodynamically. A model with a strongly cambered wing therefore stalls, and lands, at a lower airspeed. A glider with well cambered wings will be capable of tighter turns at low flight speeds. At negative angles (inverted flight), the reverse is the case: the cambered profile, at negative aerodynamic angles, stalls before the symmetrical one.

The modeller often can only guess at the angle of aerodynamic zero, so the layout of rigging angles of incidence usually depends mainly on experience rather than any very refined calculations.

3.12 Camber and drag

The camber of a wing has an important influence on drag at different angles of attack, and hence on performance. A strongly cambered wing will achieve its minimum drag at high angles of attack (low speed), but will be inefficient at low angles, i.e., in high speed flight (Figure 3.18). Conversely, a wing with slight camber will operate effectively at small angles of attack but will tend to stall early. For each type of camber there is a best or *ideal angle of attack*. If the camber is increased (for instance by lowering a flap), the angle of attack for least drag will be increased, and vice versa.

If efficiency is of importance, matching of camber to application is essential. For a given aircraft, the weight and 'G' loads to be sup-

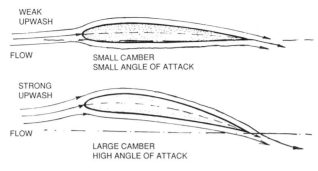

WEAK
UPWASH

FLOW

SMALL CAMBER
SMALL ANGLE OF ATTACK

STRONG
UPWASH

FLOW

LARGE CAMBER
HIGH ANGLE OF ATTACK

Figure 3.18 The ideal angle of attack

ported are the same and the power available is determined by the engine used. The lift forces required from the wing are the same. The camber alters the profile drag price paid for this lift. If, at some particular speed and trim, the drag is a minimum, more efficient flight results. In a pylon race, for instance, or a sailplane speed task, the angle of attack is very small. It is important to have minimum profile drag at this low angle of attack. This means using a profile with very low or even zero camber. The aeroplane will stall, and land, at higher airspeed than an exactly similar type with more camber but for racing the increased difficulty of handling is compensated by a greater maximum flight speed. (Flaps might be lowered to make landing easier.) Conversely, if the model is to fly efficiently at low speeds, as a sailplane when soaring is required to do, then the ideal angle of attack of the chosen wing section should be high, meaning a greater camber. (Flaps to vary the camber of multi-task sailplanes are very common.) The average club sports model flier is probably not greatly concerned with maximum performance, so the choice of camber is less critical. Even so, there are distinct differences in flight between wings of different camber and the sports flier will notice these in practice. Two otherwise similar models with wings of different camber will handle differently.

The first thing to find out about any wing section, therefore, is its camber. If this is not stated with the plans of the model or on the ordinates of the aerofoil section itself, there are various ways of working it out or measuring it. These are described in more advanced texts.

3.13 The camber of NACA four digit aerofoils

Some aerofoil designers make it very easy to determine the camber. The well known American *NACA 'four digit'* aerofoils, which are still very useful for ordinary models, have a statement about the camber in the first two digits. The first figure gives the amount of camber in percentage terms, so that the *NACA 4412, 4425, 4320, 4510* profiles all have 4% camber, the *2409* has 2% camber, the *6409,* 6%, the *0010* zero camber (symmetrical) and so on (Figure 3.19).

The second digit gives the point in tenths of the wing chord where the camber reaches its highest value. Thus in the examples above, the *NACA 4412* reaches its maximum of 4% camber at 40% of the chord, the *4425* the same, the *4320* reaches 4% at 30% chord, the *4510,* 4% at 50% chord, the *2409,* 2% at 40% and so on.

The last two digits refer to the thickness of these profiles in percent, as discussed below.

3.14 Thickness forms

In choosing an aerofoil, after the camber the basic thickness form should be considered. The camber line has already been likened to the thin wing which lies within every thick section, or the skeleton around which the 'flesh' of the wing is arranged. Various other ways of describing the structure of a wing section may be useful. The section may be thought of as a symmetrical shape or *thickness form* which has been bent to fit the camber line. Every aerofoil section, whatever its origins, can be regarded as a symmetrical form married to a selected camber line. When a section is shown on a plan, or even when the modeller plots it from a table of ordinates, it may not immediately be apparent that the shape does result from the bending of a thickness form to a camber line, but it is so.

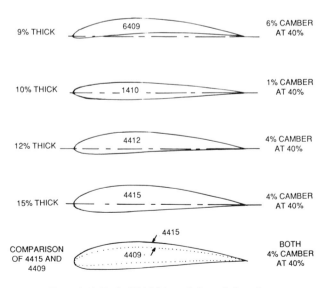

Figure 3.19 Typical NACA four digit aerofoil sections

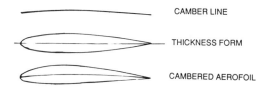

CAMBER LINE

THICKNESS FORM

CAMBERED AEROFOIL

**Figure 3.20 Formation of cambered profile by combining
camber line with symmetrical thickness form**

A series or family of different aerofoils can be constructed from any one profile as a starting point. The *NACA 4 digit* family is a famous example. A certain type of camber line was chosen, with variations of camber amount and chordwise maxima, but essentially all the same type of curve. Then a preferred thickness form was designed, variable in percentage thickness but otherwise the same basic shape on each occasion. The basic ordinates of the outline were scaled up or down as required. Every *NACA 4 digit* profile represents the marriage of this type of thickness form with this type of camber line (Figure 3.20).

The *NACA 4 digit* thickness form was based on many studies of streamlined flow in wind tunnels and flight tests during the first thirty years or so of heavier than air flight. The shape so discovered was employed for all sorts of things, including objects as large as airship hulls and as small as streamlined section struts and wheel fairings. This basic shape gave *low profile drag* and was not much affected by small imperfections in the surface (Figure 3.21). In all cases, to produce an *NACA 4* digit symmetrical form of one thickness is a matter of simply multiplying the ordinates of any of the other symmetrical forms by an appropriate factor. Thus, a 10% form can be found by multiplying the ordinates of the 5% thick form by 2, or by multiplying the 20% thick form by 0.5, or by multiplying the 2% form by 5 and so on. Thus, the *NACA 6409, 4409, 2309, 5609* profiles all use the same thickness form which is the *0009*, 9% thick form. The *0012*, 12% thick form and the *0015* are the same but with the ordinates increased, the *0004* thickness form would have the ordinates reduced and so on for all this very large family of profiles.

Other researchers at the same time arrived at almost exactly similar symmetrical and cambered sections. Most of the later Gottingen profiles, for instance, can be matched quite well to equivalent *NACA 4 digit* profiles, and the same goes for the British aerofoils produced by the Royal Aeronautical and National Physical laboratories, French Eiffel sections and most others from this period. If the camber and thickness forms are similar, there is very little to choose between the aerofoils from these differing sources. Other families of profiles from

ORDINATES

NACA 0009 LE RADIUS 0.89 PERCENT

CHORD STATION XU	UPPER SURFACE YU	CHORD STATION XL	LOWER SURFACE YL
0.000	0.000	0.000	0.000
.600	1.010	.600	-1.010
.800	1.170	.800	-1.170
1.250	1.420	1.250	-1.420
2.500	1.961	2.500	-1.961
5.000	2.666	5.000	-2.666
7.500	3.150	7.500	-3.150
10.000	3.512	10.000	-3.512
15.000	4.009	15.000	-4.009
20.000	4.303	20.000	-4.303
25.000	4.456	25.000	-4.456
30.000	4.501	30.000	-4.501
40.000	4.352	40.000	-4.352
50.000	3.971	50.000	-3.971
60.000	3.423	60.000	-3.423
70.000	2.748	70.000	-2.748
80.000	1.967	80.000	-1.967
90.000	1.086	90.000	-1.086
95.000	.605	95.000	-.605
100.000	.095	100.000	-.095

NACA 0010 LE RADIUS 1.10 PERCENT

CHORD STATION XU	UPPER SURFACE YU	CHORD STATION XL	LOWER SURFACE YL
0.000	0.000	0.000	0.000
.600	1.120	.600	-1.120
.800	1.250	.800	-1.250
1.250	1.578	1.250	-1.578
2.500	2.178	2.500	-2.178
5.000	2.962	5.000	-2.962
7.500	3.500	7.500	-3.500
10.000	3.902	10.000	-3.902
15.000	4.455	15.000	-4.455
20.000	4.782	20.000	-4.782
25.000	4.952	25.000	-4.952
30.000	5.002	30.000	-5.002
40.000	4.837	40.000	-4.837
50.000	4.412	50.000	-4.412
60.000	3.803	60.000	-3.803
70.000	3.053	70.000	-3.053
80.000	2.187	80.000	-2.187
90.000	1.207	90.000	-1.207
95.000	.672	95.000	-.672
100.000	.105	100.000	-.105

NOTE: THE ORDINATES FOR ANY OTHER
THICKNESS ARE FOUND BY MULTIPLICATION
E.G. THE ORDINATES FOR THE 9% FORM ARE FOUND
BY MULTIPLYING THE 10% ORDINATES BY 0.9
AT 30% CHORD, THE 9% ORDINATE IS 5.002 X 0.9 = 4.501
AT 30% CHORD, THE 15% ORDINATE IS 5.002 X 1.5 = 7.503

9% 0009

10% 0010

Figure 3.21 The NACA four digit thickness form

TABLE OF NACA THICKNESS FORM ORDINATES, '6' SERIES LAMINAR BOUNDARY LAYER TYPE

NACA 63 009

Chord Station XU	Upper Surface YU	Chord Station XL	Lower Surface YL
.000	.000	.000	.000
.500	.749	.500	-.749
.750	.906	.750	-.906
1.250	1.151	1.250	-1.151
2.500	1.582	2.500	-1.582
5.000	2.196	5.000	-2.196
7.500	2.655	7.500	-2.655
10.000	3.024	10.000	-3.024
15.000	3.591	15.000	-3.591
20.000	3.997	20.000	-3.997
30.000	4.442	30.000	-4.442
40.000	4.447	40.000	-4.447
50.000	4.056	50.000	-4.056
60.000	3.358	60.000	-3.358
70.000	2.458	70.000	-2.458
80.000	1.471	80.000	-1.471
90.000	.550	90.000	-.550
95.000	.196	95.000	-.196
100.000	.000	100.000	.000

NACA 63 006

Chord Station XU	Upper Surface YU	Chord Station XL	Lower Surface YL
.000	.000	.000	.000
.050	.160	.050	-.160
.100	.240	.100	-.240
.200	.350	.200	-.350
.400	.500	.400	-.500
.500	.503	.500	-.503
.750	.609	.750	-.609
1.250	.771	1.250	-.771
2.500	1.057	2.500	-1.057
5.000	1.462	5.000	-1.462
7.500	1.766	7.500	-1.766
10.000	2.010	10.000	-2.010
15.000	2.386	15.000	-2.386
20.000	2.656	20.000	-2.656
30.000	2.954	30.000	-2.954
40.000	2.971	40.000	-2.971
50.000	2.723	50.000	-2.723
60.000	2.267	60.000	-2.267
70.000	1.670	70.000	-1.670
80.000	1.008	80.000	-1.008
90.000	.383	90.000	-.383
95.000	.138	95.000	-.138
100.000	.000	100.000	.000

NACA 64 1 012

Chord Station XU	Upper Surface YU	Chord Station XL	Lower Surface YL
.000	.000	.000	.000
.500	.978	.500	-.978
.750	1.179	.750	-1.179
1.250	1.490	1.250	-1.490
2.500	2.035	2.500	-2.035
5.000	2.810	5.000	-2.810
7.500	3.394	7.500	-3.394
10.000	3.871	10.000	-3.871
15.000	4.620	15.000	-4.620
20.000	5.173	20.000	-5.173
30.000	5.844	30.000	-5.844
40.000	5.981	40.000	-5.981
50.000	5.480	50.000	-5.480
60.000	4.548	60.000	-4.548
70.000	3.350	70.000	-3.350
80.000	2.029	80.000	-2.029
90.000	.786	90.000	-.786
95.000	.288	95.000	-.288
100.000	.000	100.000	.000

NACA 65 006

Chord Station XU	Upper Surface YU	Chord Station XL	Lower Surface YL
.000	.000	.000	.000
.500	.476	.500	-.476
.750	.574	.750	-.574
1.250	.717	1.250	-.717
2.500	.956	2.500	-.956
5.000	1.310	5.000	-1.310
7.500	1.589	7.500	-1.589
10.000	1.824	10.000	-1.824
15.000	2.197	15.000	-2.197
20.000	2.482	20.000	-2.482
30.000	2.852	30.000	-2.852
40.000	2.988	40.000	-2.988
50.000	2.900	50.000	-2.900
60.000	2.518	60.000	-2.518
70.000	1.935	70.000	-1.935
80.000	1.233	80.000	-1.233
90.000	.510	90.000	-.510
95.000	.195	95.000	-.195
100.000	.000	100.000	.000

other research organisations originated in much the same fashion. Members of the *NACA four digit* series have the advantage that camber and thickness are immediately known from the number.

3.15 Thickness and profile drag

A thick wing, other things being equal, will disturb more air than a thin one if both are at their ideal angle of attack. Hence, at this angle, matched exactly to the camber, the thick wing will be less efficient than the thin one. If an aeroplane, i.e. a racer, or a speed record model, is intended to fly always at maximum speed and everything else, including turning performance, stalling and landing characteristics, is sacrificed to this one ambition, the fastest model will be the one with the thinnest possible wing. In practice, a crashed racer will not win races, so the model builder compromises, accepting a slightly lower maximum speed for the sake of safer flight in turns and easier landing and take off. The wing will therefore be thicker than that which would produce the absolute minimum drag for the sake of absolute maximum speed. A model which handles safely and puts in a reliable performance every time it flies is likely to win many more races than one which has to be flown very accurately all the time, to keep the angle of attack within the very narrow limits of a thin aerofoil.

A model which must perform well over a very wide range of angles of attack, such as an aerobatic model and a cross country or multi-task sailplane (without flaps), must represent a more difficult compromise. As mentioned already, the thicker wing section works quite well over a wide range, but its minimum profile drag is always greater than a thin section at the ideal angle. For aerobatics, models with wing sections about 15% thick have proved very suitable, and since maximum airspeed is not particularly important, the increase of profile drag caused by thickness is acceptable. Full-sized sailplanes using the older type of aerofoils, such as the NACA 4 digit series and equivalents from Gottingen, commonly used to fly with aerofoils about the same thickness, 15%. For models, thinner profiles are usually preferable, because scale effects are more severe with aerofoils more than 10 or 12% thick (see 3.19)

3.16 The profile drag bucket

One way of expressing the difference between thick and thin wing sections is to speak of the *low drag range* or *drag bucket* (Figure 3.22). When the profile drag of a wing is measured, it is found that the minimum drag occurs at the ideal angle of attack, but there is a range on either side of this where there is little change. On the resulting graphs of profile drag against lift, the drag curve takes a bucket-like

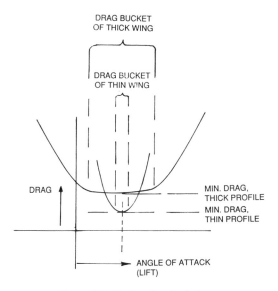

Figure 3.22 The low drag bucket
of thick and thin wings

shape. If the bucket is wide, the range of angles of attack which can be used is large, and if the bucket is narrow, a critical situation is found: the section works well only at its best angle. Thick sections have wide but rather shallow drag buckets, thin sections have deep but narrow drag buckets. The wide drag bucket means that at angles of attack far from the ideal, profile drag will actually be lower than the wing with a narrow but deep drag bucket. This is a much better situation for the sports model or for the multi-task sailplane which must often fly at very slow, as well as very fast, airspeed. Some modern full sized sailplanes, for this reason, have wing sections 17 and 19% thick, and 21% has been used in the past. Models do not perform well with such thick wings, unless very large in chord and fast in flight.

3.17 Thickness and lift
Because the airflow over a thickish, rounded leading edge is less prone to separate at high angles of attack than over a sharper nose, the thick wing as a rule continues to give useful lift at angles of attack where a thin profile of exactly similar camber begins to stall. Hence thick wings are in some respects high lift wings and make for slower landing and take off speeds. As before, the less experienced pilot will do better with somewhat thicker profiles than the expert who demands a higher performance and can handle somewhat 'hotter' aircraft.

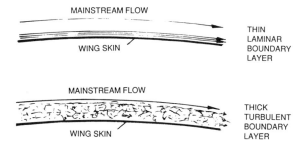

Figure 3.23 Laminar and turbulent boundary layers

3.18 Laminar and turbulent flow

In search of lower drag, much attention has been given, in recent times, to the flow of air within the boundary layer, the layer of air which is dragged along by friction with the skin of the wing rather than simply flowing past it. The boundary layer is often decisive in deciding when a wing stalls, since separation begins first in this layer. Within the boundary layer, two very different kinds of flow occur, laminar and turbulent (Figure 3.23).

A *laminar* boundary layer is one in which the flow near to the skin of the wing is arranged in very thin sheets or laminae which slide smoothly over one another with very little frictional resistance. A laminar boundary layer creates little skin drag. A *turbulent boundary* layer is very disturbed, particles moving up, down and sideways rapidly. This creates more frictional drag on the wing surface. The turbulent boundary layer is also thicker than a laminar one, so the general streamlined flow outside the boundary layer has to pass over what is, in effect, a thicker shape than if the boundary layer is all laminar. This increases form drag.

On full-sized aircraft, the boundary layer over a wing usually begins laminar, but after a very short distance, the smooth sliding flow breaks up and the boundary layer becomes turbulent (Figure 3.24). A rough

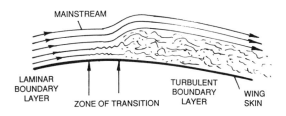

Figure 3.24 Boundary layer transition
on full-sized aircraft

visual impression of what happens may be obtained by observing the way water spreads out over a smooth surface, such as a bath or sink bottom, when a tap is turned on. The flow is laminar at first, but at some distance from the point where the jet of fluid strikes the surface transition occurs and turbulent flow, with an increase in depth, prevails. The boundary layer over a wing, although invisible, closely resembles this. Once transition takes place, the process cannot be reversed, so high skin drag continues on a wing aft of the transition, all the way to the trailing edge. (Experiments have been done with suction through small holes in the wing, to remove the turbulent boundary layer after it forms. This can restore laminar flow, but it soon changes again to turbulent. The suction has to continue to the trailing edge.)

Quite small defects, such as rivet heads and barely detectable dimples in the wing skin, fly specks and paint chips, can spoil even the small amount of laminar flow that exists. Hence full-sized aircraft often fly with fully turbulent boundary layers.

3.19 Scale effects
A few centimetres behind the leading edge of a large aeroplane the boundary layer usually becomes turbulent. Although the skin drag is high, at least the main airflow is not forced away from the surface. Model wings behave differently from full-sized ones in this respect. On a model wing, the few centimetres of laminar flow may extend from the leading edge to some point quite well aft on the wing, how far depending on the *chord* of the wing at each point, and the *speed* of flight. This at first sounds as if a model should have an advantage, in terms of profile drag. Unfortunately this is not the case. A laminar boundary layer on a model wing, just because it does create less skin drag and has less transfer of flow energy to the wing, tends to separate from the surface altogether as soon as the point of minimum pressure (maximum flow speed) is passed. In the worst case, this separation is total. The wing stalls very early. Slow free flight models with thick

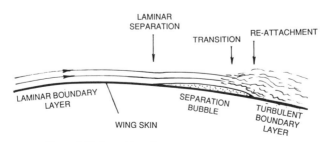

Figure 3.25 Formation of separation bubble

wings and small chords suffer from such premature stalling and perform badly. With radio controlled models, if the wing is not too thick, what normally happens is the formation of *separation bubbles* (Figure 3.25).

When the laminar boundary layer leaves the wing skin, after a short delay it usually breaks up into a turbulent layer, which is thicker. This increase of thickness allows it to reattach to the wing. Underneath the separated area is a 'bubble' of stagnant air which does not move downstream with the flow, but remains on the wing, with a circulation of its own. The separation bubble may be several centimetres long in the chordwise direction, and on a small model may cover most of the upper wing surface. There will usually be a lower surface bubble too.

The larger the wing, and the faster it flies, the less important these separation bubbles become. They do occur on full sized sailplanes, but on a large wing at high flying speed, a small separation bubble has little influence. On a model wing, flying slowly with small chord, such a bubble can cause a very serious deterioration in performance. It creates an effective disturbance to the mainstream airflow and this creates additional form drag. The effect of a separation bubble may be likened to opening a small airbrake, a few millimetres high, all the way from wing tip to wing tip, on the model. Model wings are therefore never as efficient as full sized ones.

3.20 Turbulators

It sometimes improves the performance of a small chord, slow flying model if the formation of a separation bubble can be prevented by triggering boundary layer transition before the minimum pressure point is reached on the wing. This can sometimes be done by using *turbulators* (Figure 3.26). These are very thin strips of narrow tape, stuck onto the wing spanwise, some small distance ahead of the point where the separation bubble would be expected to develop. The turbulator should not be too thick, since if it is so, it might have a worse

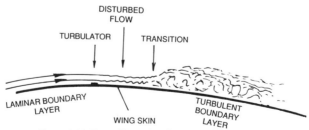

**Figure 3.26 Forced boundary layer transition
with turbulator**

effect on performance than the separation bubble itself. There is some evidence to suggest that laying the tape in a fine sawtooth or zig zag fashion produces a greater effect. It is also thought by some model fliers that using a slightly rough wing covering material, such as fabric lightly doped, instead of very glossy film or paint finish, helps to bring about boundary layer transition. Very little definite information is available here as a guide, but turbulators are worth trying if there is any doubt about the performance of a particular model. The tape strips can be placed in position and removed fairly easily, and the resulting change in model behaviour observed. The idea of using several turbulators or boundary layer *invigorators* one behind the other is also worth investigation. The intention is not to promote turbulent flow over the whole wing, but to preserve the laminar boundary layer over the forward part of the skin as far as it is safe to do so, then to cause transition just before the laminar separation point. Turbulators may be worthwhile on both upper and lower wing surfaces and experiment is, at present, the best means of finding out where they should be placed.

The separation bubble problem is only one aspect of the scale effect. Another problem is caused by the inherent viscosity of the air. Movement through viscous fluids, like treacle, is much more difficult than through less viscous substances like water or air. Although air is not very viscous, none the less it has a certain stickiness. For a very large aeroplane, this is relatively unimportant, but for small creatures, such as gnats and midges, flying is extremely difficult. To such small wings the air seems almost like treacle. To compensate, small insects beat their wings at extremely high rates, so the rate of airflow over their surfaces is quite high. Model aeroplanes come between these extremes, not so small as insects, but not so fast as full-sized aeroplanes. In relation to size of wing and speed, the relative viscosity of the air increases drag at all times. The fast flying model with large wing chord always has an advantage over the small, slow one with narrow chord for this reason, quite apart from the separation bubble effects mentioned above. Viscosity effects are felt more strongly by thick wings, which is another reason for using thin aerofoils on models, when minimum drag is required.

The scale effect is often expressed in terms of the Reynolds *number* or Re. Full-sized powered light aeroplanes fly at Re numbers greater than 1,000,000, sailplanes and ultralight aeroplanes rather less than this at their lower speeds. Pylon racing models and multi-task sailplanes reach Re about 500,000 at their maximum speeds and widest wing chords. Most sports models fly at Re about 100,000 up to 300,000. Gnats and other small insects are down in the 5 to 10,000 Re range.

3.21 Modern wing sections

In efforts to obtain more laminar flow over the wing, new wing sections, beginning with the *NACA '6'* series, were developed. (The first digit is the figure 6, and there are at least 6 digits in the aerofoil number, e.g. 646–612.) The first application in practice was on the *P 51 'Mustang'* fighter of World War 2. Providing the wing with one of these profiles is accurately made, free from small waves or humps and depressions, clean and without chips or blobs in the paint work, it is possible to extend the region of laminar boundary layer back to the point on the wing where the pressure reaches its minimum (maximum flow speed). Transition to turbulent flow occurs just behind the point of maximum thickness on the wing. The thickness forms used for all modern wing profiles, therefore, have the maximum thickness point further aft than the old, turbulent flow type. The shape of the extreme leading edge, which must be carefully rounded to a precise nose radius, is also of great importance (Figure 3.27).

Since the early *NACA '6'* series, more refined profiles, especially those designed by Wortmann, Eppler, and others, have sought to extend the benefits of laminar boundary layers. On full-sized sailplanes, boundary layer control by blowing or suction through small holes in critical places is also very common, air being 'piped' to such points from special intakes or extractors.

Because perfect accuracy is rarely achieved, and since aircraft actually in service are hardly ever kept scrupulously clean and free of surface damage, the benefits of the new thickness forms are hardly ever fully achieved in practice. In economic terms, it costs a great deal of money to produce a perfect wing and to keep it clean in use. This high cost is not necessarily regained in service despite greater efficiency. Hence many full-sized light aeroplanes still have exposed rivet heads, dimples and waviness in the overlapping metal skins, and fabric covering which sags between ribs. All these prevent laminar flow in the boundary layer but enable the aircraft to be cheaply produced and easily maintained in day to day operations.

Where the wing can be made more perfect, very large improvements in performance are possible. Full-sized sailplanes, with wings in moulded plastic reinforced by various fibres, cleaned afresh before every flight, have improved vastly as a result of these discoveries. Even so, during a long flight, especially when flying at fairly low altitudes, the wing picks up the crushed bodies of many insects, which break up the laminar boundary layer. Rain drops produce effects very like opening an air brake.

For models, many specially designed aerofoil sections are available, having been devised to allow as far as possible for scale effects.

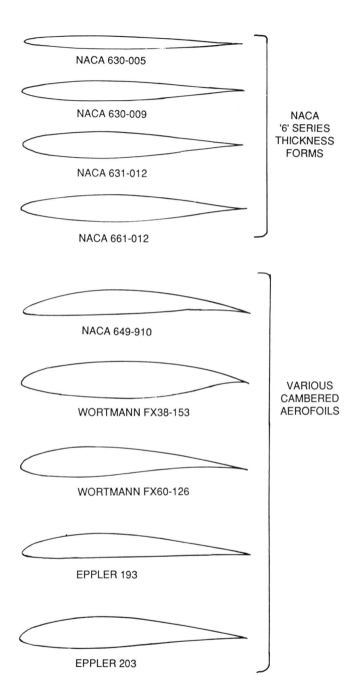

Figure 3.27 Some modern aerofoils

These profiles all depend on accuracy in construction and careful maintenance of the wing surface. It is not good enough, with such profiles, to use a traditional type of model structure with an open framework and a plastic or fabric covering which is sure to sag somewhat between ribs or spars. The wing skin must be supported everywhere and great care must be taken to ensure that the profile is accurate, the surface free from waves and ripples, and smooth. Even such small defects as paint lines where masking tape has been used to make a colour change on the wing can disturb a laminar boundary layer. The use of turbulators has already been mentioned but there is a great difference between the careful placement of a turbulator and the accidental disruption of a laminar flow boundary layer by a carelessly applied paint finish or set of transfers. Dedicated contest model fliers spend a great deal of time and trouble producing accurate wings, using moulding techniques very similar to those for full-sized sailplanes. The results are good, but it is not certain that the wing profiles themselves are responsible. Wind tunnel tests reveal that the theoretical expectations for these wing sections are rarely achieved even with perfectly accurate test pieces. If made with similar care, wings with more traditional profiles may perform just as well. Much remains to be discovered here.

Except for the most advanced contest fliers, the ordinary, old-fashioned wing profile is perfectly adequate and may be used with confidence. It remains important, always, to choose a suitable camber and thickness. If these are well judged, there is very little to go wrong. A NACA 4 digit profile, always identified by its camber and thickness, will give good results. Although it is always best to build the wing carefully, a profile of this type will be uncritical of small errors and will tolerate a certain degree of waviness and covering sag. To use a laminar profile and then build it with some imperfections is actually worse than to use an old fashioned aerofoil.

4 THE WING IN PLAN

4.1 Wing area

The most important fact about any wing is its total area, since upon this depends its total aerodynamic reaction with the air at any flight speed and angle of attack. Area is expressed in terms of 'square' measures such as square metres, square feet, or often in modelling, square decimetres or square inches. It would probably be better if, in future, the standard *Systeme Internationale* were used everywhere, since in the long run this would avoid such confusion. In this system the square metre is the standard unit of area.

There are some conventions used when describing the area of a model aeroplane wing. Most models have fuselages and some have engine nacelles and other attachments which interrupt the outline of the wing. The lines of the wing are projected onto a horizontal plane and extended in the simplest possible way through fuselages and nacelles (Figure 4.1). The area enclosed by the projected lines is counted as part of the wing. In all but a very few cases this gives an accurate idea of the total supporting surface, but there are exceptions. Some aeroplanes and sailplanes have very carefully shaped fuselages which are designed to act as wings to some extent. To ignore

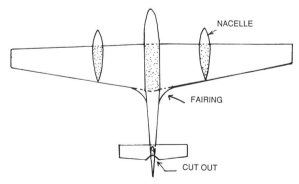

Figure 4.1 The area of a wing includes portions
effectively buried inside fuselage or nacelles
but normally does not include fairings or cut outs

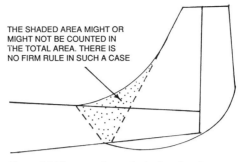

THE SHADED AREA MIGHT OR
MIGHT NOT BE COUNTED IN
THE TOTAL AREA. THERE IS
NO FIRM RULE IN SUCH A CASE

**Figure 4.2 The area of a vertical tail surface is
often difficult to determine**

the effective increase in total supporting area would be misleading. On the other hand, to include a mere wing root fairing in the total area, even if it is larger than usual, is also misleading since the support obtained from such a feature is usually negligible. Some judgment has to be used and where there is any doubt, the simplest approach is usually the safest. There may, particularly on scale models, be cut-out segments. These should be excluded from the total wing area.

The same rules apply to other horizontal surfaces such as stabilisers, for example where an elevator has a substantial cut-out to allow the rudder to move. Establishing the area of vertical fins is quite difficult since these often blend smoothly into the fuselage. Since the rear fuselage is itself often fairly deep and narrow it may act to some extent as a fin. As before, the simplest method of projecting the fin area through the fuselage is the best but there is often room for argument (Figure 4.2).

Where a stabiliser is arranged in V form, the equivalent horizontal area is found by projecting the outline onto the horizontal plane. (That is, the plane containing the X and Y axes of the aircraft.) In the side view of the model, the area appears projected onto the vertical plane

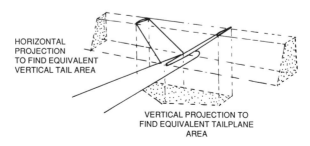

HORIZONTAL
PROJECTION
TO FIND EQUIVALENT
VERTICAL TAIL AREA

VERTICAL PROJECTION TO
FIND EQUIVALENT TAILPLANE
AREA

Figure 4.3 Projection to find area of V tail

but this should be doubled to allow for the hidden part of the unit (Figure 4.3).

In model aviation, some difficulty arises because of a decision taken many years ago by the controlling body for sporting aviation, the *Federation Aeronautique Internationale (FAI)*. At the relevant time, free flight models were almost the only type existing, and the duration of each flight was all-important. Some contest modellers attempted to increase their seconds in the air by using very large 'lifting' tailplanes, hoping to gain extra lift without corresponding drag. Models which were nominally of a certain wing area actually had much larger horizontal surface area because the tails were inflated so much. This practice probably did not gain the contestants any real advantage. As noted in earlier chapters, any lifting surface creates its full share of drag. Merely increasing the total lifting surface does not necessarily produce a more efficient aircraft, even from the narrow point of view of duration flying. None the less, there were breaches of the spirit of the rules, so a regulation was introduced to prevent such tactics. Ever since, for all contest and record purposes, the nominal supporting surface area of all model aircraft has included the area of all wings and projected stabilising surfaces. In full-sized aviation this is not usually done unless the aircraft is designed all through as a canard or tandem type in which the total supporting area does include the stabiliser. In almost all ordinary models, the mainplane alone (set of mainplanes in biplane and triplanes) is the effective supporting component and the stabiliser is, as its name implies, only there to trim and stabilise the mainplane.

4.2 Wing loading

When the area of the wing is known, the next most important point is to establish the total weight to be supported by this area. As emphasised in the opening chapter of this book, the strength of any aerodynamic reaction force depends on the speed and size of the object moving through the air. To support a given weight at a given angle of attack, either a small area of wing may be moved fast through the air or a larger wing may produce the same force at a slower speed. Hence the relation of area to weight relates directly to the speed of flight. This relationship is expressed as the *wing loading,* usually stated in *SI* units as kilogrammes of mass relative to wing area in square metres, or in modelling circles either as grammes per square decimetre or ounces per square foot.

A model which is heavy in relation to its wing area will have a high wing loading and, other things being equal, will have to fly fast in order to support itself. Fast flight requires large thrust, so a model with high wing loading will require a powerful motor in relation to its wing area. A model with large wing area and small weight, with low wing loading, will fly slowly because the large wing will generate enough lift force at low airspeed.

When two or more models are built from the same plans or from similar kits, they will not differ in wing area but may be of different weight. They will then have different wing loadings and will fly at different speeds. If a model builder is very careless, using heavy wood, being too lavish with heavy adhesives and perhaps applying too many thick coats of paint to the finished aircraft, the model may be considerably over weight and will then require more engine power to enable it to perform in a satisfactory way. This is especially likely if the extra weight of paint or wood at the rear end, for instance, makes it necessary to add yet more weight at the front of the model to bring the balance point to a safe location (ahead of the neutral point, see Chapter 5). Increasing engine power usually means employing a larger motor, which in turn tends to increase the wing loading still further. The lighter powered model generally flies better and has a greater reserve of thrust in hand, enabling more manoeuvres and aerobatics to be flown.

4.3 Ballast in sailplanes

Sailplanes often carry ballast to increase their weight and wing loading, in order to fly faster. The additional weight causes the glider to descend at a greater rate, so where flight duration is important, the ballast may be removed. In many situations, however, a fast glide is more important than a slow rate of sink (Figure 4.4).

It can be shown by simple arithmetic that if a glider is flying through sinking air towards an upcurrent, it is much better to fly fast, even though this means coming down rapidly. When trying to penetrate through a downcurrent, the glider with a high wing loading will reach the upcurrent sooner and higher and will begin to climb, while the lightly loaded sailplane is still floating gently along, lingering in the sinking air. It is much more important to get the model into the lift than to keep the rate of sink to its minimum while passing through bad air. Modern full-sized sailplanes usually carry very large quantities of water ballast for this reason and jettison the water only if the upcurrents become very weak. Best results come if very high airspeeds are used in the straight glides through sinking air, often twice or three times the airspeed for the nominal best L/D ratio. The same applies to models. Even though the heavy sailplane climbs more slowly, it will still be higher than the light model when this finally arrives in the upcurrent - if it ever does! The time advantage gained by the heavy model in the fast glide is rarely made up by the light one in the climb,

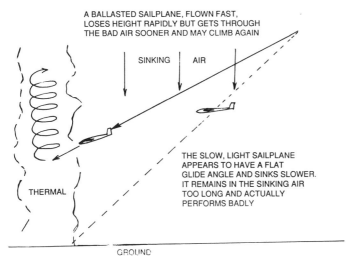

A BALLASTED SAILPLANE, FLOWN FAST, LOSES HEIGHT RAPIDLY BUT GETS THROUGH THE BAD AIR SOONER AND MAY CLIMB AGAIN

SINKING   AIR

THE SLOW, LIGHT SAILPLANE APPEARS TO HAVE A FLAT GLIDE ANGLE AND SINKS SLOWER. IT REMAINS IN THE SINKING AIR TOO LONG AND ACTUALLY PERFORMS BADLY

THERMAL

GROUND

Figure 4.4 The effect of ballast and fast glide on a sailplane

so sailplanes with fairly high wing loadings generally perform better all round than the ultra lightweights. There is a limit to this, of course. A sailplane which was so heavy that it could not soar in anything but a very strong and wide upcurrent would always be on the ground. A compromise is necessary. In weather with very weak upcurrents and correspondingly feeble downcurrents, the lightly loaded sailplane succeeds

In a speed task for the International F3B class of contest, duration is of no importance, the model being required to fly very rapidly over a measured course (at the time of writing, four laps of a 150 metre course, 600 metres total distance). This is done by taking a high, fast launch to start the flight, then diving to gain more speed and entering the task in a steep gliding descent. Ballast enables the models to achieve very high velocities, although the necessity to turn the glider at the end of each lap tends to restrict the total of additional weight carried (see 4.4 below).

4.4 Turning at high wing loadings

A model with high wing loading, at a given angle of bank, requires a larger radius to achieve the same rate of turn as a light one (Figure 4.5). This is of great importance. In all turns, the mass of the aircraft is acted on by accelerations which multiply the loads on the wing. To accomplish the turn, the wing has therefore to provide a greater lift force than in level flight. This, as usual, increases the drag, so requir-

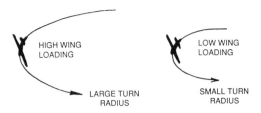

Figure 4.5 The effect of wing loading on
radius of turn. Models of equal size, at
the same angle of bank

ing more thrust to keep the airspeed up. In a powered aircraft, this must come from the engine. With a glider, it can be obtained only by steepening the angle of descent, i.e., losing more height than the pilot would like. Whenever a glider turns, its rate of sink increases, and if the wing loading is high, this effect becomes more pronounced. At the same time, the larger turn radius caused by high wing loading may take the model out of the thermal in which it is soaring. In a race or speed task, the heavily loaded model is compelled to fly a greater distance when turning. This inevitably tends to reduce the average speed.

4.5 Span loading

After wing area, wing span is the next most important feature of a wing in plan. The span is simply the total distance from extreme tip to extreme tip of the wing, including any portion of the surface which lies within the fuselage, nacelles, etc.

It is worth considering the weight of the model in relation to its total wing span, to arrive at its span loading. The span loading may be expressed as so many kilogrammes mass to so many metres of span, or so many pounds weight to feet of span. In general, if the span loading is low, and the wing loading and wing areas are equal, the low span loading aircraft will fly faster on a given power, or, if it is a sailplane, will achieve a better gliding performance, than one with high span loading.

4.6 Aspect ratio

A convenient way of expressing the relationship of wing span to wing area is the aspect ratio. This requires a simple calculation. The span of the wing is divided by the mean or average chord, to arrive at a figure such as 6 : 1, which would be the aspect ratio of a fairly typical powered model, or 20 : 1 which might be found on a sailplane (Figure 4.6). Some full-sized sailplanes have aspect ratios greater than 35 : 1. An alternative method of finding the aspect ratio of a wing, which is

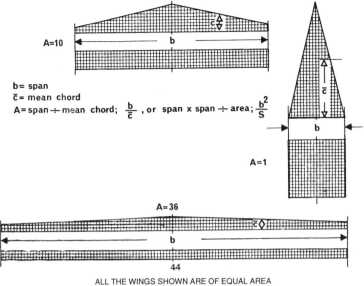

b = span
c̄ = mean chord
A = span ÷ mean chord; $\frac{b}{\bar{c}}$, or span x span ÷ area; $\frac{b^2}{S}$

ALL THE WINGS SHOWN ARE OF EQUAL AREA
BUT OF WIDELY DIFFERING ASPECT RATIOS

Figure 4.6 Aspect ratio

useful where the shape is complicated, is to square the span (i.e., multiply it by itself) and divide the result by the area. (Use consistent units - square metres with metres, square feet with feet, square inches with inches, etc.)

4.7 Vortex drag

Increasing the aspect ratio is a very important means of reducing *vortex drag*. (Sometimes called *induced drag*.)

Whenever a wing or other surface is generating lift, as noted above, there is a difference in air pressure above and below the wing. At the tips, therefore, the air tends to flow from the lower, relatively high pressure side, round the tip to the low pressure area above. This tendency biases the flow outwards on the under side of the wing and inwards above, and the influence extends towards the centre sections of the wing so that everywhere on the wing, except in the very centre, the air does not flow directly from leading edge to trailing edge. There is some sideways inclination of the flow on the underside, outwards towards the tips, and on the upper side, inwards towards the root. When the upper and underside flows meet and merge at the trailing edge, they are travelling in slightly different directions. When two layers of fluid shear across one another in this way, numerous small vortices form and these trail off like many twisted threads (Figure 4.7). Behind the wing, therefore, there is a sheet of vortices. These rapidly spinning threads of air absorb a great deal of energy and the wing feels this as a drag force, the *vortex drag.* The more lift being demanded from the wing, the more pronounced this effect, so the vortex drag is especially large whenever a model aircraft is flying at a high angles of attack, e.g., in turning flight, tight aerobatics, and when coming in to land or taking off. It should also be noted that a stabiliser, when required to produce a lift force, also produces vortex drag. There is no way in which a stabiliser can be persuaded to give a little extra lift without incurring a drag penalty. Any surface which generates lift generates vortex drag in flight, the more the lift, the more the vortex drag.

Since the cause of all the vortices is the wing tip, where the high and low pressure areas are close together, the cross flows in the airflow become greater over the outer panels of the wing and the strongest vortex forms just behind the tip. This vortex is so strong that it very quickly twists all the others into itself, so that some small distance behind the wing, the entire sheet of thread vortices is wrapped into the main vortex, which trails behind the aeroplane for a considerable distance before finally being slowed down and re-absorbed into the general airflow (Figure 4.8). With very large aeroplanes taking off and landing at airports, the trailing vortices, created by their wings at high angles of attack, can often persist for several minutes and if a light aeroplane flies into such a rotating airstream it may be thrown completely out of control.

Since the tip is the cause of vortex drag, the effect of aspect ratio on drag can be appreciated. The further apart the tips are, for a given wing area, the less their influence on the flow over the main part of the wing. There is no way of avoiding tip vortices altogether. They exist because a lifting wing must have high and low pressure sides and where these come together there will be cross flows, but by stretching the span, the total power of these cross flows is reduced greatly. For a given wing area and angle of attack, doubling the aspect ratio actu-

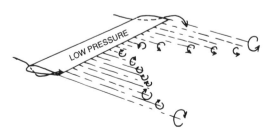

Figure 4.7 The vortex sheet behind
a lifting wing

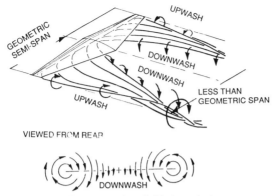

VIEWED FROM REAR

Figure 4.8 The vortex sheet behind a real wing

ally halves the vortex drag. The effect is most significant at high angles of attack. Sailplanes invariably fly at high angles of attack when soaring, which is the reason for the high aspect ratios of these aircraft.

For the ordinary sport powered model, which rarely needs to fly efficiently at high angles of attack, vortex drag is much less important and so high aspect ratios are not necessary. It is very difficult to design and build a high aspect ratio wing which will be strong and stiff enough for safety, and also light. Modern sailplanes, as mentioned already, are not worse off for being heavily loaded, except when upcurrents become very feeble. Hence designers have accepted the penalties of extra weight and have generally built sailplanes with very large spans relative to their wing areas. Along with the large span and mass of such wings come many other difficulties. The flexibility of long, slender wings is quite alarming. (The wing tips of some modern full-sized sailplanes flex up and down several metres under changing loads and, in a heavy landing, both tips may touch the ground together.) Flutter, the uncontrollable twisting back and forth of the wing, is also much more likely with a high aspect ratio.

For most powered model aircraft, it is better to have a wing of moderate span which can easily be made light and strong. Such a light wing responds more rapidly to controls and is less likely to flutter than a high aspect ratio type.

4.8 Vortex Induced Downwash

The trailing vortices have a very important influence on the general airflow around the aeroplane, both behind the wing and in front of it. Since air is a fluid, and the airspeed of models is much less than the speed of sound, any large disturbance of flow, such as a powerful vortex, is felt by the air for large distances in all directions. The air ahead

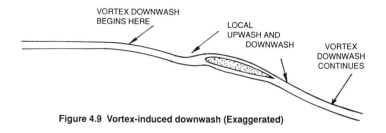

Figure 4.9 Vortex-induced downwash (Exaggerated)

of an approaching aeroplane begins to feel the trailing vortices and responds. *Before the wing arrives,* the vortex induces a downward slant to the flow. The air is already inclined at a downwash angle when it reaches the neighbourhood of the wing. The *vortex induced downwash* reduces the angle at which the airflow arrives at the wing, altering the angle of attack, often by several degrees. Whatever the angle of attack measured relative to the flight path of the aeroplane may be, the vortex downwash reduces this to some extent. The effect is more pronounced when the vortices are strong, as they are with a low aspect ratio wing. The basic geometric angle of attack also affects the strength of the downwash. The higher the angle of attack, the stronger the downwash tending to reduce it.

Behind the wing, downwash continues everywhere between the trailing vortices. The aerodynamic angle of attack of the tailplane, if any, is altered, how much depending on the angle of attack of the mainplane and on the precise position of the tail. In the case of a canard or tandem layout, the trailing vortices of the front wing reduce the aerodynamic angle of attack of the rear one. In turn, because the downwash extends both fore and aft of any lifting surface whatever, the aerodynamic angle of attack of the foreplane is reduced by downwash from the rear plane. All these effects may be calculated or

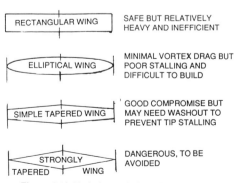

Figure 4.10 Variations of wing planform

estimated. Where the figuring is not done, previously successful aircraft of similar type may be used to give a good indication of suitable rigging angles.

With the canard or tandem type of layout, it is very important that the trailing vortices of the forewing should not strike the rear plane. If they do, not only is the airflow over the rear plane greatly disturbed, reducing lift and increasing drag, but vibration and structural problems also arise. Usually, the foreplane is placed relatively low to allow the vortices to pass below the rear plane.

4.9 Refinements of the wing plan

It was shown by early aerodynamic theorists, and confirmed by many practical experiments in flight and in wind tunnels, that the total strength of all the vortices created by a lifting wing, and hence the vortex drag, could be reduced if the wing had a perfectly constant distribution of vortex induced downwash from root to tip. This could be achieved by making the wing of elliptical planform (Figure 4.10). Since the ellipse is really a circle which has been stretched, this is perhaps not very surprising. (Strictly, a circle is a special case of the ellipse.) The rotating vortices causing downwash, and the general circulation pattern of air round a wing, accommodate best to a wing which is itself related to the circle in plan view. With an elliptical planform, the downwash is of equal strength across the whole span, so the true aerodynamic angle of attack everywhere is the same. Every part of an elliptical wing then contributes its fair share of lift. The lifting work is evenly shared by the whole area, and the vortex drag price paid is also equally spread and at its minimum. When this became fully understood by aircraft designers, many full-sized aeroplanes, and some models, appeared with elliptical wings. The *Spitfire* is a well known example.

The elliptical wing is not easy to build. Small penalties caused by departure from the perfect form may be accepted. Sailplanes, as usual, are designed to be as efficient as possible even at some additional cost, so the planform of their wings is almost always very close to the ellipse, even if this means double or triple forms of tapering. It is believed by some theorists that when a wing is tapered, the trailing edge outline should be straight, with changes of taper confined to the leading edge. Some modern sailplanes have adopted this form.

Aircraft which normally fly fast, at low angles of attack, have very little to gain aerodynamically by having elliptical wings, since the vortex drag is low anyway. Simply tapered wings at high speeds lose very little in drag compared with the ellipse. Because of their greater depth at the root, tapered wings are lighter, as a rule, than those of rectangular plan, so tapering is usually advantageous even when there is not much to be gained from the drag point of view. Even when, for reasons of simplicity and cheapness in construction, rectangular wings are retained, rounding the tips, or making these roughly elliptical, produces substantial savings in vortex drag. It is thought to be best to keep the trailing edge straight, and round the tip by turning the leading edge back.

4.10 Swept wing effects

Sweep back or forward of a wing in plan has some effect on vortex drag. Generally, sweep decreases efficiency, although if the angle of sweep is small the effect is not noticeable in practice. Large angles of sweep, either back or forward, are used for full-sized aircraft either to improve balance or because sweep is advantageous when flight speeds approach the velocity of sound.

Some full-sized two seat sailplanes have used swept wings in order to give the pilot in a rear cockpit a better view. If the wing were straight on these aircraft, the rear pilot's seat would be within the wing root area and the wing would greatly hamper the outlook. Sweep forward allows the wing root to be placed behind the seat while keeping the aerodynamic centre of the wing close to the rear cockpit (Figure 4.11). Fast subsonic and supersonic aircraft benefit from sweep, either for-

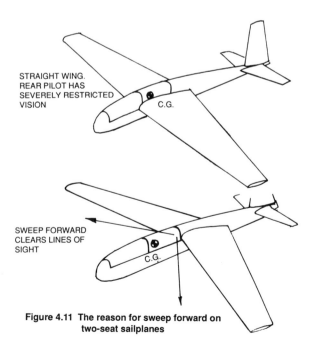

STRAIGHT WING.
REAR PILOT HAS
SEVERELY RESTRICTED
VISION

C.G.

SWEEP FORWARD
CLEARS LINES OF
SIGHT

C.G.

Figure 4.11 The reason for sweep forward on
two-seat sailplanes

ward or aft, because the critical Mach number is reached later, on such wings, and when the shock wave forms, the sweep keeps most of the wing out of its immediate influence.

4.11 Gaps and leaks

Emphasis on the planform of the wing directs attention to the effect of such things as cut-outs and gaps. If a wing has a chordwise gap of any appreciable size, the effect is almost equivalent to an extra pair of tips (Figure 4.12). Wherever such a gap occurs, air will stream through from high to low pressure side and a strong vortex will form. Sealing the gap, even with a simple strip of tape, can make a very large difference to the performance of the model. Chordwise gaps are always to be avoided, if possible. Gaps along control hinge lines often reduce the effectiveness of the control surface behind them.

Cut-outs and other irregularities of shape also have bad effects, especially near the wing roots. Biplanes often have cut-outs in the wings, to give the pilot a better view or to increase the field of fire for guns. On scale models these will be imitated but they do have a considerable effect on performance. This sacrifice was accepted, in the

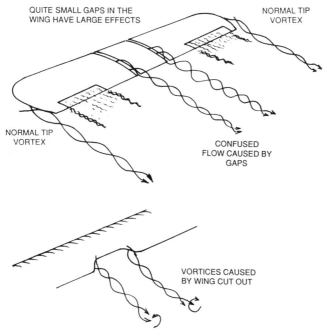

Figure 4.12 The effects of gaps and cut outs on wing drag

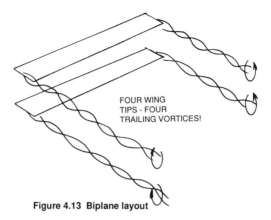

FOUR WING
TIPS - FOUR
TRAILING VORTICES!

Figure 4.13 Biplane layout

prototypes, because an aircraft which has to be flown by an almost sightless pilot is not much use to anyone. The cut-outs, none the less, should be recognised for what they are. Aerodynamically they have bad effects wherever they appear.

4.12 Multiplane layouts

Biplanes have the advantage of concentrating a large area of wing in a small span. The two wings can be braced together to make a very strong and stiff structure with little weight. They proved very successful in the early decades of aviation when flight speeds were low and engine power not very great. The small span of the total aeroplane allowed very rapid rates of roll to be achieved and the low wing loading permitted turns to be flown on small radius, all advantages in a fighting aeroplane, or one intended for aerobatics. The same applied to triplanes and multiplanes with more than three sets of wings, one above the other. Unfortunately, to divide a given area of wing into two or

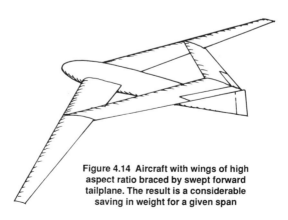

Figure 4.14 Aircraft with wings of high aspect ratio braced by swept forward tailplane. The result is a considerable saving in weight for a given span

more mainplanes multiplies the number of wing tips and wing tip vortices. Hence the drag of all such aircraft is excessively great at high angles of attack. This is inherent in the layout and is not merely a result of the struts, wire bracing and mutual interference of the one wing with the other. These are additional causes of high drag. The biplane (or multiplane) layout is inefficient, in drag terms, at low speeds because of the tip vortices, and at high speeds because of the very large parasitic drag of struts, wires, etc. Hence when engine power increased and flight speeds became greater, the monoplane wing was soon recognised as the most efficient, despite its greater weight and span. Speed proved more important than turn ability, in the long run.

Much of what has been said about biplanes applies also to tandem aircraft where the lift is shared more or less equally between fore and rear sets of mainplanes. Four tips create four tip vortices, and hence a substantial increase in vortex drag, especially when the aircraft is at a high angle of attack.

For certain special purposes, the tandem layout is useful, when, for instance, large changes of centre of gravity in flight are to be expected. As with multiplanes, some substantial reduction in structural weight can be achieved by bracing one wing to the other in some way. The Rutan *Voyager* aircraft which flew non-stop round the earth in 1986 is an example of this, and there have been successful flights by model sailplanes where a large rear wing has been used, in a diamond layout, to brace a high aspect ratio foreplane (Figure 4.14). Some home built aeroplanes have also taken advantage of this layout. Small span is often very important if an aeroplane is to be built and housed in a restricted space. A tandem layout with the wings joining at the tips in a diamond pattern is compact and strong, yet light.

4.13 Wing tip stalling

The equal downwash effect of the elliptical wing has been noted. When such a wing approaches the stalling angle of attack, the whole surface, from tip to tip, arrives at this critical angle together and the result is a sharp stall, often with little warning to the pilot. In practice, one side reaches the stall a fraction before the other. This causes a sharp roll towards the stalled wing, often followed by a spin. For this reason, the perfectly elliptical wing is less safe than a planform which has a greater chord towards the tips. Frequently, while the designer follows a close approximation to the ellipse over the inner parts of the wing, the tip is made somewhat squarer. The resulting modified ellipse is nearly as efficient as the more perfect form, but tends to stall at the root first, the separation then spreading out laterally, avoiding the dangerous 'wing dropping' roll.

4.14 Washout

Sometimes, in order to achieve a very light structure, an extreme form of taper may be used, so that the wing tips are narrower than those of the ideal elliptical form. This is very dangerous. The effect is to overload the wing tips, requiring them to produce more lift than their area allows. The principle of equal work sharing, area for area, of the elliptical form, operates against the narrow tip. When the stalling angle approaches, the overworked wing tips stall before the root. Such a wing always tends to drop a wing very sharply when stalling and may catch the pilot unprepared.

To prevent wing tip stalling in tapered wings, one commonly used device is *washout,* which is the geometrical reduction of the angle of incidence of the outer part of the wing (Figure 4.15). The wing is built deliberately with a twist to reduce the angle of incidence of the outer panels. This is very effective, and can transform a dangerous tip stalling wing into one that is perfectly safe. Unfortunately, to do this disturbs the approximately elliptical load distribution, so increasing drag. When such a wing is flying at different angles of attack, the load sharing across the span changes because of the washout. In particular, at high speeds, when the angle of attack of the root of the wing is very small, the washout brings the tips to zero or even less than zero, aerodynamically. This causes the tip panels to 'lift' downwards while the rest of the wing is lifting normally, upwards. This download on the tips bends the outer wings down. The additional load has to be made up by more lift over the inner wing panels. The result is a considerable increase in drag and serious loss of efficiency. On a racing model or a high speed, multi task sailplane, wing twist is to be avoided if possible. It is much better to use a less tapered planform and do without any washout. (*Washin,* twisting the wing to a greater angle of incidence at the tip, promotes tip stalling and should not be done unless there is some over-riding reason for it. Warps introduced accidentally during construction of the wing should also be avoided but if they do occur, washout is less dangerous than washin at the tips.)

Other ways of preventing tip stalling are feasible and are used on full-sized aircraft and some models. The wing tip aerofoil section may be different from that at the root, with a gradual change from the inner to the outer wing panels. If the tip profile is chosen for its late stalling character, even with a sharp taper, the root section may stall first, as required. To be sure of achieving this result, wind tunnel test results, at the appropriate Reynolds number, are really necessary.

Carefully designed slots in the leading edge, or auxiliary slats which open when the wing is near the stalling angle, delay the stall by allowing air from the high pressure area just below the leading edge of the

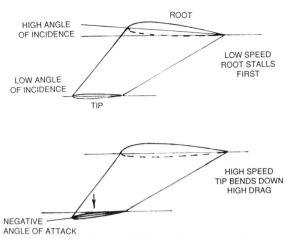

HIGH ANGLE OF INCIDENCE

ROOT

LOW SPEED ROOT STALLS FIRST

LOW ANGLE OF INCIDENCE

TIP

HIGH SPEED TIP BENDS DOWN HIGH DRAG

NEGATIVE ANGLE OF ATTACK

Figure 4.15 Washout to control stalling

wing, to pass through and produce a stream over the upper surface. The energy of this fast flowing air enables it to remain attached to the wing, delaying or preventing flow separation (Figure 4.16).

4.15 Winglets and tip sails

Ever since it was realised that the wing tips cause serious increases of drag, efforts have been made to prevent or reduce the wing tip vortices. The first attempts involved fitting large flat plates, vertically, at the tip. This does achieve some reduction in vortex strength, but air pressure changes are communicated from one place to another around whatever obstruction is put in the way. The high pressure region under the wing extends down on the inside of any tip plate, the low pressure zone on the upper surface, is felt at the top of the plate. Air therefore tends to flow around the tip plate, and the vortex, although weakened, does not vanish. At the same time, the air flows over the

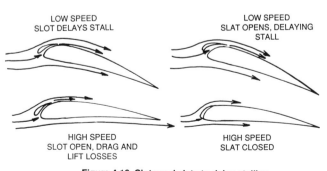

LOW SPEED SLOT DELAYS STALL

LOW SPEED SLAT OPENS, DELAYING STALL

HIGH SPEED SLOT OPEN, DRAG AND LIFT LOSSES

HIGH SPEED SLAT CLOSED

Figure 4.16 Slots and slats to delay stalling

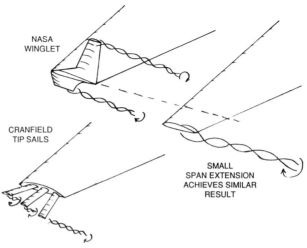

Figure 4.17 Winglets and tip sails

whole surface of the plate and this creates additional skin friction and form drag, so tending to reduce the total benefit. Tip plates of this simple form have not proved useful in practice.

More recently, various forms of *winglet* and *tip sail* have been developed and these have been applied with success to both full-sized and model aircraft (Figure 4.17). The idea of these devices is not merely to restrict and weaken the vortices, but to extract energy from them and use it to provide a useful additional forward-directed force. The net effect is a reduction of vortex drag, especially at low

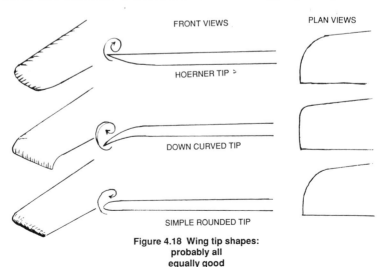

Figure 4.18 Wing tip shapes: probably all equally good

flight speeds and high angles of attack. Correct placement and design of the winglets is necessary if their benefit is to be realised. Badly placed, they do more harm than good.

Again, the existence of the appendages increases the skin and form drag of the wing, so the full gain is not achieved. What is perhaps more important is that if the wing is extended in span, with a plain tip, it is easy to reduce the vortex drag by increasing the aspect ratio. In terms of structural complications, cost and simplicity of design, this is usually a better method of reducing vortex drag. Winglets find their most promising application when there is a strict limit on the total wing span of an aircraft, as is the case with some classes of model sailplanes in competition. Adding a well designed winglet, extending vertically upwards at the tip, does reduce vortex drag without increasing the total wing span, and so the model remains within the contest rules.

4.16 Wing tip shapes

If winglets or sails are not used, there is really very little that can be done to reduce tip vortex drag, other than careful design of the wing in plan, and some attention to the detail of the wing tip itself. There is very little evidence to show that any one type of wing tip is noticeably superior to any other. Some designers have tried to restrain the tip vortex by bending the tip downwards (Figure 4.18). Others, notably Hoerner, advocated a slight upsweep, this being intended to carry the vortex outwards and allowing it to form just beyond the tip. In fact, neither up nor down sweep of the extreme tip has been shown to make any real difference. The trailing vortex in any case does not form at the tip, but slightly behind it. At the tip itself, the flows are inclined at several degrees to the direction of flight, but the main vortex develops behind the wing and slightly inboard. A well shaped tip may improve the airflow over the outermost part of the ailerons and winglets probably have a similar effect but many of these gains remain to be proved.

Probably the best way of dealing with wing tips is to round them off in a simple fashion, to reduce skin friction and form drag as far as possible, and accept that the trailing vortices will be present.

4.17 Locating the aerodynamic centre of a wing

As mentioned in the previous chapter, the aerodynamic centre of a wing profile is always very close to the quarter chord or 25% position, measuring from the leading edge. In plan view, if the wing is entirely without sweepback or forward with respect to the quarter chord point at every place across the span, the aerodynamic centre of the whole wing or stabiliser will lie at 25% of the root chord. A rectangular wing, for example, will have its a.c. at this point.

Very few wings are actually completely free of sweep. Often a slight sweepback is used, to ensure that the main spar, set at right angles to the centre line, runs through the thickest part of the aerofoil. In other cases, the wing may have a complicated shape in plan. It sometimes becomes necessary to calculate or measure the position of the wing aerodynamic centre, since the placement of the centre of gravity relative to this point has a marked effect on stability and balance. A simple construction that may be used with straight tapered wings is illustrated (Figure 4.19). With complicated shapes, methods of calculation are given in more advanced texts. For most practical purposes, the modeller can estimate with a fair degree of accuracy where the mean wing chord lies relative to the wing root, and the aerodynamic centre of the whole wing then lies at 25% of this.

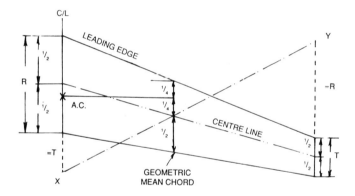

STEPS
1. DRAW TO SCALE A HALF PLAN OF THE WING, WITH ROOT CHORD R AND TIP CHORD T
2. DRAW THE CENTRE LINE FROM MID POINTS OF TIP AND ROOT
3. EXTEND THE ROOT CHORD BACK BY AN AMOUNT EQUAL TO T AND EXTEND THE TIP CHORD FORWARD BY AN AMOUNT EQUAL TO R
4. JOIN THE ENDS OF THE EXTENSIONS, X-Y
5. WHERE THE LINE X-Y CUTS THE CENTRE LINE MARKS THE POSITION OF THE MEAN CHORD
6. ONE QUARTER OF THE MEAN CHORD FROM THE LEADING EDGE IS THE AERODYNAMIC CENTRE OF THE HALF WING
7. PROJECT THIS POINT TO THE AIRCRAFT CENTRE LINE TO FIND THE WING AERODYNAMIC CENTRE

**Figure 4.19 Finding the aerodynamic centre
of a simple tapered, swept wing**

5 STABILITY

5.1 What stability is

There is probably no subject in model aeronautics which is so frequently misunderstood as stability, so it is best to begin with a basic statement.

An aircraft is stable if it tends always to settle down in the flight attitude which the pilot commands by use of the controls.

To stress the point, if a model is to be flown inverted, the pilot will roll, or perhaps half loop, the aeroplane, and then hold the controls in an appropriate position to retain the inverted attitude. An aeroplane which is stable when inverted will strive to keep this attitude as long as the controls are kept in the required position. An unstable aircraft will not do this, so the pilot will have to work hard all the time just to keep the aircraft as it is. Many models which are stable when right way up become unstable inverted. Trainers and many sport flying models are usually very stable when upright but unstable when inverted so that if the inexperienced pilot makes an error the model will automatically try to return to normal, upright, flight. Aerobatic models are often designed to be stable both upright and inverted.

In the same way, a model which is stable in a steep climbing attitude with the throttle set for the required power will tend to continue in the steep climb so long as the controls and power are set for this. The same in a dive; the stable model will continue diving at a constant angle and speed when trimmed that way and not otherwise.

It is possible to fly an unstable aircraft but it requires very great skill with instantaneous, and correct, action by the pilot in every moment. This is extremely exhausting and in practice even the most expert pilot will have great difficulty in avoiding a crash. The unstable model will not hold any position and requires constant control actions. Flying an unstable model may be likened to balancing a ball on an inverted round bowl. (Neutral stability is like controlling a ball on a perfectly flat surface. See 5.6.)

It follows that if the pilot takes no action the stable model will try to take up whatever flight attitude it is trimmed for. Most model fliers set

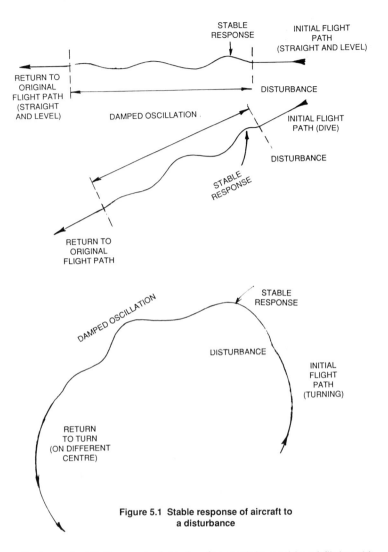

Figure 5.1 Stable response of aircraft to
a disturbance

up their ccntrol linkages and angles for straight and level flight with centralised controls but this is a matter of convenience, not necessity. Free flight models are often trimmed for a steady turn and radio controlled models with 'fail safe' devices may be the same. Whatever position the controls are in, the stable model will respond accordingly.

The beginner who becomes disoriented is often advised to let go of the controls entirely. The springs in the transmitter are usually arranged to centralise the controls (except the throttle), if released. If the model is stable and trimmed for upright flight with controls neutral, it will sort itself out and take up this position. Recovery takes some

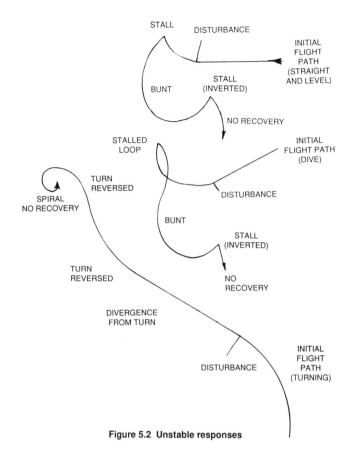

Figure 5.2 Unstable responses

time. If a model is in some extreme attitude such as a vertical dive or spin, centralising the controls will tend to bring it out of this dangerous situation but there may not be sufficient altitude for the complete recovery to take place.

Models which are stable with respect to one of the three axes (X, Y or Z, see Chapter 2) may be unstable about one or both of the others. The fully stable aircraft is stable about all three. Since the air itself is seldom perfectly calm, even a very stable model will never hold its attitude perfectly. There will always be some small, or large, deviations from the pilot's wishes. A gust may strike the model, tending to upset it, or the pilot may unintentionally 'twitch' the controls and cause a small change. After any upset, the model usually tends to swing to and fro, oscillating dynamically before settling down. The stable model therefore does not follow a perfectly smooth flight path. For example, if a gust causes the model's nose to rise slightly, a stable model will respond by pitching the nose down but this motion usually goes a little too far. The stability will then raise the nose again, but this, while not being as severe as the initial disturbance, will also go a little too far and will be followed by a nose down pitch, and so on (Figure 5.1). A satisfactory model will damp out the oscillations fairly quickly and will return to the original position, but quite possibly another gust or upset of some kind will happen and the result will be further oscillations. A model which oscillates in this way shows *static stability.*

In similar circumstances, an unstable model will respond to any disturbance by exaggerating it (Figure 5.2). There will be no regular oscillations but simply divergence. Thus, a small nose up pitch caused by a gust will find the unstable aircraft pitching even more nose up into a stall. The pilot may be able to prevent this by using the controls. However, as soon as the model responds to the corrective control by pitching nose down, since it is unstable it will immediately try to pitch even more nose down, possibly 'bunting' over into the fully inverted attitude. Again, the pilot may be able to prevent this but as before, every change is instantly exaggerated by the instability and flying such a model is extremely difficult. It can be done, but has little to recommend it. The unstable model, left to itself, simply veers off course, up, down, to the side, or in any direction, and makes no attempt to return to its original position.

It is possible, though rather rare with models, to have static stability combined with *dynamic instability* (Figure 5.3). In this condition, the oscillations on either side of the desired position tend to increase instead of damping down. To prevent this, a certain excess of static stability is needed to provide damping, and the extremities of the model (tail and outer wings) should be kept as light as possible.

5.2 Stability and control

It is possible to have too much stability. If a model aircraft is too stable, it will respond to controls very slowly. This may at first seem beneficial if the aircraft is a trainer, but all aircraft get into dangerous attitudes sometimes and need rapid and firm control response to escape from them. For instance, a strong gust of wind may pitch even a very stable

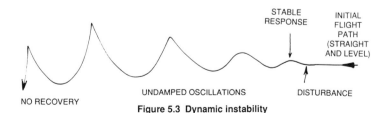

Figure 5.3 Dynamic instability

model into a steep dive near the ground, and this will require quick correction by the pilot. The in-built stability of the model may not be enough to ensure recovery before hitting something. In the same way, a model may be flying towards an obstruction such as a tree, so a quick response to turning controls is required.

Compromises are necessary. The unstable model is always dangerous, but is very sensitive to control movements. The over-stable model will probably survive longer, but is unsatisfactory because it tends to be sluggish. Somewhere between these extremes, the individual pilot will find the degree of stability that seems most suitable for the particular model and the kind of flying the pilot prefers. Someone who enjoys aerobatics will prefer a model with just enough stability to yield consistency and predictability, but rapidity of response will be essential. The margins of stability on such aircraft will be quite small. The model flier who prefers a gentler, more relaxed style will opt for increased stability at the expense of somewhat less sensitivity.

5.3 Stability in pitch

It was explained in Chapter 1 above that any aeroplane or glider, whatever its layout, has an *aerodynamic centre* or *neutral point* at which all the forces may be assumed to act. Providing the airflow over the main components remains streamlined, this point is fixed. It normally lies somewhere between the mainplane and stabiliser, nearer to the larger surface roughly in proportion to the respective areas. The total of all the lift forces which support the model in flight acts at this point.

Various ways of finding the neutral point of an entire aircraft are available but most model fliers do not need to know how this is done. (More advanced texts give the methods.) Suffice it to say here that increasing the area of the stabiliser tends to move the neutral point towards this surface, decreasing the stabiliser area moves the n.p. closer to the mainplane. Removing the stabiliser entirely, as with a tail-less design, shifts the neutral point to the aerodynamic centre of the wing, at 25% of the mean wing chord position. Other factors affecting the location of this point include the aspect ratio of the mainplane and stabiliser, the distance or moment arms between the two surfaces, the stabiliser efficiency, and other factors such as the position of the wing wake at different angles of attack.

Increasing the distance between the stabiliser and the mainplane is equivalent to an increase of stabiliser area, because the forces on the stabiliser then have greater leverage or moment arm (Figure 5.4). In the case of orthodox aircraft with tailplanes, if the fuselage is very short the tail tends to lose effectiveness because it lies in the region of

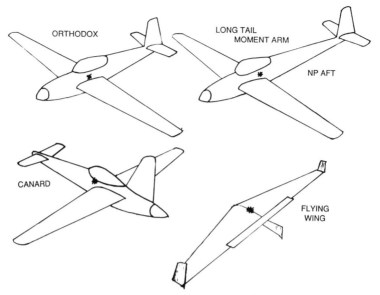

Figure 5.4 Location of the neutral point
* marks position of neutral point

disturbed air behind the wing. Increasing the tail moment arm is thus beneficial for stability in two ways, increasing leverage and increasing tail efficiency. A tailplane may sometimes be mounted high, as with a 'T' tail layout, to get the stabiliser out of the wing wake (Figure 5.5). A tailplane which is at the end of a rather wide fuselage tends to be relatively ineffective. Some of its nominal area is buried inside the fuselage itself, and the surface exposed is within the disturbed air produced by the fuselage wake itself.

As noted in the previous chapter, the tail is also affected by the wing's vortex-induced downwash and requires a different angular

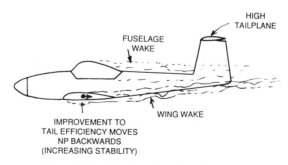

Figure 5.5 The 'T' tail configuration takes the tailplane out of the wing and fuselage wake, improving its effectiveness

setting to give the same balancing effect, depending on the strength of the vortex downwash in its neighbourhood.

The tail-first or canard layout takes the forewing completely out of the wing wake, with a good effect on its power. (The forewing is still within the influence of the mainplane's vortex-induced downwash. See 4.8 above.) The wake of the forewing reduces the efficiency of the mainplane, though not, as a rule, very greatly unless the tip vortices strike the wing.

The fuselage and other components of an aircraft, such as engine nacelles, usually tend to shift the neutral point of the whole slightly forward.

5.4 Centre of gravity location

As the angle of attack of the aircraft changes in response to gusts etc., at a given flight speed, the resulting variation of lift force is felt at the neutral point. An increase in angle of attack produces an increase of the lift force and a reduction of the angle produces a reduction of the lift. The pitching stability of an aircraft is almost entirely determined by the position of the centre of gravity in relation to the neutral point where these changes of lift force act. Any surface, such as wing, forewing, or fuselage, which has its aerodynamic centre ahead of the centre of gravity tends to destabilise the model, and any such surface aft of the c.g., tends to stabilise it.

Almost all pitch stability and elevator control problems can therefore be overcome by *adjustment of the centre of gravity position*. It is very easy to change the centre of gravity, much harder to alter the neutral point position since this involves changing the areas of wings and stabiliser, and perhaps altering the length of the fuselage.

Moving the c.g. forward, by adding ballast to the nose of the model, increases stability. Moving the c.g. aft reduces stability and, if carried too far, can produce serious instability. The pilot should experiment with c.g. position to find the degree of elevator response that suits the model and the pilot's taste. There is no single answer. The pilot's preference is the decisive factor.

Every change of c.g. position requires readjustment of the elevator trim for straight and level flight (Figure 5.6). Moving the c.g. forward increases the total nose down pitching moment. This is balanced out by setting the elevator and/or stabiliser at a new angle, i.e., adding nose up trim. *This change does not shift the neutral point.* In the same way, moving the c.g. aft requires a different elevator angle, without altering the neutral point location.

It must be emphasised again that altering angles of incidence and elevator trim does not change the location of the neutral point, although changes of centre of gravity position do require new trim settings. Putting this the other way round, if a model is unstable in pitch, or too stable, altering the angular settings will not improve the situation. The centre of gravity should be adjusted, *after* which trim changes will be required.

With orthodox aircraft, if the centre of gravity is located exactly at the 25% mean chord point of the wing, as it often is, a small tailplane will provide adequate stability and will easily trim out the pitching moments to ensure balance. Such a placement renders the wing neutral in stability, so the small tailplane, well aft of the centre of gravity, is a powerful stabilising surface and does not have to fight against the wing during any disturbance.

If the c.g. is aft of the 25% mean wing chord position the wing will tend to destabilise the model. A larger tailplane will be required to

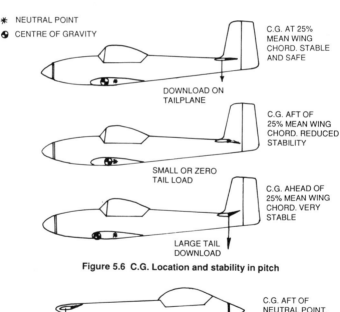

Figure 5.6 C.G. Location and stability in pitch

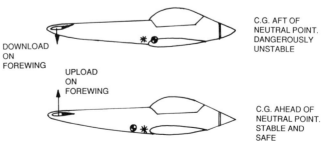

Figure 5.7 Stability and instability of a canard layout

counteract this. This is a common arrangement with model aircraft. Very frequently, the c.g. is placed at about 30 to 35% of the mean wing chord. The tailplane then has to be enlarged to give adequate stability. In most cases, a more forward c.g. with smaller tail (of similar efficiency) would be equally satisfactory. A small tailplane with c.g. at 25% of the mean wing chord gives the same static stability in pitch as a larger tailplane with c.g. at 35%. (See the discussion of *static margin*, section 5.7 below.) Putting this, too, another way, if a model is not stable enough, increasing the tailplane area will make it more stable but moving the c.g. forward will have the same effect, with less trouble.

If the c.g. is ahead of the wing quarter chord point, stability will increase. Flight in this forward c.g. trim is very safe except that it may tend towards the over-stable condition. To prevent this, the tailplane may be reduced in area. This kind of arrangement has enabled some scale models of full-sized aircraft with very small tails to be made more stable.

With a canard layout, if the centre of gravity is aft of the neutral point the aircraft becomes almost uncontrollable. It is very important to note that the neutral point of a canard is ahead of the mainplane's aerodynamic centre. For stability and controllability the c.g. must be ahead of this neutral point, which takes it, usually, somewhat forward of the mainplane's leading edge. When this is done, the canard is

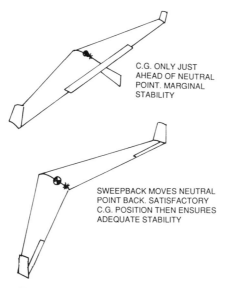

C.G. ONLY JUST
AHEAD OF NEUTRAL
POINT. MARGINAL
STABILITY

SWEEPBACK MOVES NEUTRAL
POINT BACK. SATISFACTORY
C.G. POSITION THEN ENSURES
ADEQUATE STABILITY

Figure 5.8 Stability of an 'all wing' aircraft

perfectly stable and safe in the longitudinal sense. To call the foreplane a stabiliser is actually an over-simplification. Since it lies ahead of the centre of gravity, it actually de-stabilises the aircraft, although necessary for balancing out the pitching forces. The wing, aft of the c.g., becomes the stabiliser. (Figure 5.7. Difficulties of lateral stability may remain.).

With a 'flying wing', the c.g. must be ahead of the wing's aerodynamic centre, which is effectively the neutral point of the whole aircraft (Figure 5.8). Tailless aircraft can be made quite stable and controllable in pitch, providing the c.g. is well forward. This requires fairly large upward elevator trim for balance, or, alternatively, the use of sweepback and wing twist, or reflex aerofoil sections, or, sometimes, all these. The result is a good deal of extra drag and poor lift characteristics at high angles of attack. Tailless aircraft nearly always tend to disappoint their designers in practice, because either they are inefficient (despite losing the drag and weight of the tail) or they are unduly sensitive to the controls and critical of centre of gravity misplacement.

5.5 How pitch stability acts

The reason that c.g. position is so important in longitudinal stability is that any change in angle of attack, producing a variation of the lift force, will either be counteracted or increased, depending on whether the c.g. is ahead of or behind the neutral point of the aircraft.

Assume the aeroplane is trimmed, which is to say, all pitching moments are zero with the elevator, throttle, etc., held still. The total lift force at the neutral point then supports the model and there is no out of balance pitching force tending to cause a change. In the stable case, the centre of gravity lies ahead of the centre of lift. If a change of angle of attack now occurs because of a gust in the air, it produces a change of the lift force, at the neutral point, behind the c.g. The previous balance is upset and a pitching moment arises. If the disturbance increases the angle of attack, a nose down correction is automatically applied and the model tends to return to its trimmed attitude (Figure 5.9). Similarly, if a reduction of angle of attack is caused by a gust, the lift force is reduced and this change of balance pitches the nose up, so, as before, tending to restore the original, undisturbed, attitude. It follows that *for stability in pitch, the centre of gravity must be ahead of the neutral point.* The further forward the c.g. goes, the greater the stability and the less sensitive the elevator control.

If the c.g. is aft of the neutral point, the situation is unstable because if an increase of angle of attack occurs, the lift force increases and this

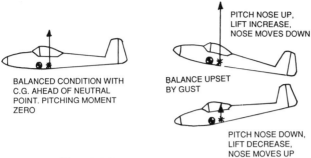

Figure 5.9 How pitch stability acts

raises the nose, exaggerating the unbalanced condition, and vice versa, a nose down disturbance finds the lift force less and the nose of the model is allowed to go further down. *Placing the centre of gravity too far aft produces an unstable model* (Figure 5.10).

5.6 Neutral stability in pitch

If the centre of gravity is exactly at the neutral point, changes of the lift force acting there have no effects on pitch. Disturbances are neither corrected nor exaggerated, the aircraft is *neutrally stable*. Whatever flight position the model happens to be in, no forces arise tending to change it unless the pilot introduces some by using the controls. (This is why the aerodynamic centre of a whole aircraft is termed the neutral point.)

Neutral stability in practice becomes almost as difficult for the pilot to cope with as instability. One cause of this is that dynamic forces also come into play. A model which is neutrally stable in the *static*

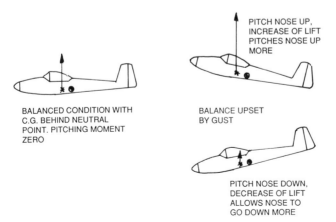

Figure 5.10 Instability with aft C.G.

111

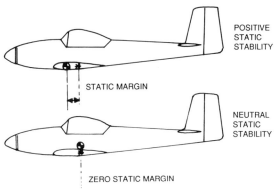

POSITIVE
STATIC
STABILITY

STATIC MARGIN

NEUTRAL
STATIC
STABILITY

ZERO STATIC MARGIN

Figure 5.11 The static stability margin

sense will usually be *dynamically unstable*. If the model is neutrally stable, there is insufficient damping. A suitable reserve or margin of static stability, obtained by moving the c.g. forward of the neutral point, is needed to damp down the dynamic oscillation.

5.7 The static stability margin

The distance between the c.g. and the neutral point is termed the *static margin* of the aircraft (Figure 5.11). This figure, given as a proportion of the mean wing chord, is a measure of how far back the centre of gravity may be shifted before the model will run into stability problems. A figure of about 0.2 or 1/5th of the mean wing chord is fairly typical for sprightly sports powered model aeroplanes. In other words, if a model has a mean wing chord of 20 cm., if the centre of gravity is moved aft from its proper position by 1/5th of 20, i.e., 4 cm., the aeroplane will become unstable. Even a movement of 1 cm. will have a noticeable de-stabilising effect. Increasing the static margin to 0.25, requiring a 1 cm. forward movement of the c.g., will make such an aircraft more docile and may be very helpful for the first few flights with a new model, until the pilot has gained experience with it. After that, some trials with aft c.g may be made to establish the right 'feel'.

Since the static margin is expressed as a simple proportion of the mean wing chord, it follows that a wide range of layouts and centre of gravity positions can produce the same static margin and the same effect, as far as stability and control in pitch are concerned. For instance, a very large tailplane with a c.g. well aft might produce a static margin of 0.2. The same figure could be achieved with a much smaller tailplane and the c.g. at 25% of the wing mean chord, or an even smaller tailplane with the c.g. further forward still. In each case the tail trim angle required would be different, but the stability would be the same.

The only limitation is to remember that tailplanes differ in efficiency. A tailplane which lies too close to the wing may suffer from the wing wake. A 'T' tail may be more effective than an ordinary, low mounted one behind a fat fuselage, and so on. Generally, such effects are small, so most models which fly well with an aft c.g. and large tail would fly equally well with forward c.g. and smaller tail. For canards, the same applies. A canard with c.g. forward and small forewing may have the same static margin, and be just as stable in pitch, as an orthodox aircraft. Tailless aircraft too achieve the same stability as other types if their static margins are the same. The static margin in all cases can be adjusted by shifting the c.g. back (to reduce stability) or forward (to increase it).

5.8 Stability in yaw

Although stability in yaw is fairly easy to understand and achieve, it really needs to be considered together with rolling stability, since, in flight, rotations about the vertical Z axis and about the fore to aft X axis invariably interact on one another. They also affect the pitching motions of the aircraft about the crosswise Y axis.

Yawing stability is equivalent to the stability of a weathercock or wind vane which always tends to align itself with the airflow (Figure 5.12). As usual, there are some oscillations before the aircraft settles down after a disturbance, just as a weather vane will swing about, but the tendency is for the stable aeroplane to keep itself aligned with the general flow direction. The vertical stabilisers of the aircraft are intended only to keep the centre line of the aircraft aligned as accurately as possible with the direction of flight. Their function is to hold a zero angle of attack in the lateral sense and prevent, as far as possible, any unwanted rotations about the vertical, Z, axis. Small departures from this alignment do not cause serious problems, but if the angle of yaw is more than a few degrees to either side, the airflow over the fuselage usually separates, in effect turning the whole of this large

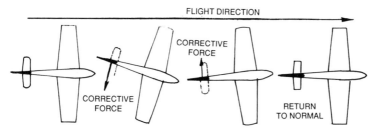

Figure 5.12 Yaw or 'weathercock' stability

113

component into an airbrake (Figure 5.13). This also often causes 'blanketing' of parts of the wing and horizontal stabilising surfaces, since these may lie within the very turbulent air coming from the separated zone. The result may be equivalent to a severe stall of one part of the wing or stabiliser. The outcome is often rather unpredictable.

As before, a stable aircraft will respond predictably to control. If the pilot wishes to yaw the model in a sideslip or, in aerobatics, to hold a 'knife edged' flight position with the wings banked vertically, a stable model will hold the required attitude of yaw so long as the controls are positioned for it.

If the aerodynamic centre of the aircraft in the vertical plane lies behind the c.g., any yawing disturbance will tend to be reversed. A yaw caused by a gust, for instance, creates an increase in the sideways acting aerodynamic force which rotates the model back towards the normal position. If the centre of gravity is behind the a.c., the unstable situation arises (Figure 5.14) and any yaw will be exaggerated.

The vertical stabilising surfaces thus act very much in the same way as the horizontal ones. The orthodox arrangement of the fin on most aeroplanes and gliders produces satisfactory yawing stability.

If stability in normal flight were the only criterion of importance, vertical tail areas could be smaller than they usually are. Other important factors come in, however, especially spin recovery and the need to counteract yawing forces coming from the propeller on aircraft with powerful engines. Yaw control to overcome adverse vortex drag from the wing when entering and leaving turns has been mentioned earlier (2.3 and 4, above).

The spinning case decrees that there shall be large vertical stabilising areas aft of the centre of gravity. Although methods of calculating

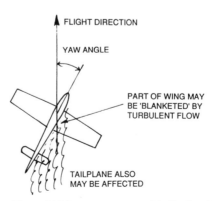

FLIGHT DIRECTION

YAW ANGLE

PART OF WING MAY BE 'BLANKETED' BY TURBULENT FLOW

TAILPLANE ALSO MAY BE AFFECTED

Figure 5.13 In a severe yaw or sideslip, the airflow separates over the fuselage, creating much drag

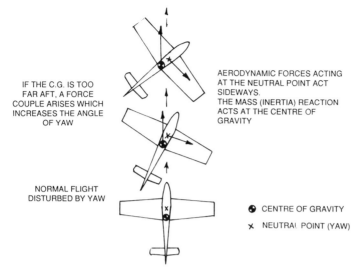

IF THE C.G. IS TOO FAR AFT, A FORCE COUPLE ARISES WHICH INCREASES THE ANGLE OF YAW

AERODYNAMIC FORCES ACTING AT THE NEUTRAL POINT ACT SIDEWAYS. THE MASS (INERTIA) REACTION ACTS AT THE CENTRE OF GRAVITY

NORMAL FLIGHT DISTURBED BY YAW

● CENTRE OF GRAVITY

✕ NEUTRAL POINT (YAW)

Figure 5.14 Instability in yaw. If the centre of gravity is too far aft, any small yawing disturbance is exaggerated

the areas are available, they do not always prove adequate in practice and experience is usually a better guide. Even in full-sized aeronautics vertical stabilisers often require modification after the early test flights.

On sailplanes in particular, the adverse vortex drag of the wing when the ailerons are used requires ample vertical stabilising areas and rudder action to ensure the aircraft enters, and leaves, the turn with little skidding or slipping.

It is quite easy to arrange a canard layout with a forward c.g. and foreplane for balance and stability in the longitudinal sense. It is very much less easy to stabilise such an aircraft in yaw (Figure 5.15). Any vertical surface ahead of the c.g. has a de-stabilising effect. Canard, tandem and 'tailless' aircraft require vertical stabilisers aft to ensure that the lateral aerodynamic centre is in the right place. However, since the centre of gravity of such layouts is usually only slightly forward of the mainplane's aerodynamic centre (25% mean chord point), the moment arm available is quite short. The 'Voyager' round the world aeroplane had its vertical stabilisers on long booms which extended aft. (The booms contained fuel.) Other canard aircraft have carried very large central fins, or have fins at the outer ends of swept back wings, to increase the effective moment arm. (These vertical surfaces at the tips are usually designed also to serve as winglets, as described in 4.15 above.) Flying wings without large vertical fins have usually proved almost uncontrollable.

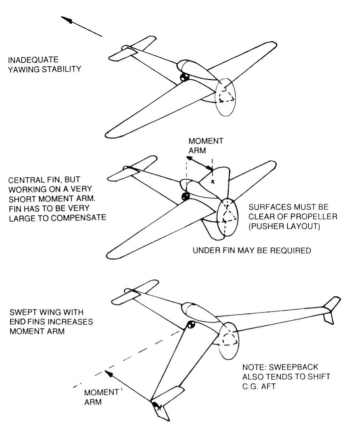

INADEQUATE
YAWING STABILITY

MOMENT
ARM

CENTRAL FIN, BUT
WORKING ON A VERY
SHORT MOMENT ARM.
FIN HAS TO BE VERY
LARGE TO COMPENSATE

SURFACES MUST BE
CLEAR OF PROPELLER
(PUSHER LAYOUT)

UNDER FIN MAY BE REQUIRED

SWEPT WING WITH
END FINS INCREASES
MOMENT ARM

NOTE: SWEEPBACK
ALSO TENDS TO SHIFT
C.G. AFT

MOMENT
ARM

Figure 5.15 Providing stability in yaw for a
canard may necessitate a large central fin,
or a swept back wing with tip fins or winglets

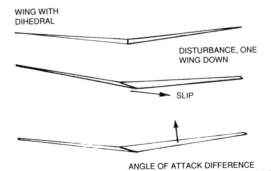

WING WITH
DIHEDRAL

DISTURBANCE, ONE
WING DOWN

SLIP

ANGLE OF ATTACK DIFFERENCE
CHANGES LIFT FORCES, PRODUCING
CORRECTIVE ROLL

Figure 5.16 Dihedral effect in roll
stability

5.9 Stability in roll; pendulum effects

A small amount of stability in roll can be obtained if the centre of gravity is below the aerodynamic centre of the aircraft. This is easiest to achieve with high wing layouts, since the weight of fuselage, engine and radio gear then is low relative to the wing. A small tilting then produces an automatic corrective force. The high wing layout is frequently recommended for trainers, for this reason. This so-called pendulum effect is relatively small unless the layout is exaggerated. When inverted, it operates the other way round, tending to roll the aeroplane upright. With low wing layouts the centre of gravity tends to be high relative to the wing, with the opposite effects on rolling stability.

5.10 Stability in roll; dihedral effects

Once a rolling motion starts, whatever the cause, the mass of the wing tends to keep the roll going. Aerodynamic forces damp the rotation down and halt it, but, once the motion stops, there will be no effort to return to the previous position. A wing is neutrally stable in the rolling sense. That is, if a gust or anything else causes the wing to bank, there will be no corrective force and it will tend to remain banked. Rolling stability can be provided by giving the wing dihedral, but only because tilting the wing causes a sideslip or skid.

When the wing is banked, the lift force is inclined to one side while the weight still acts vertically downwards. The two forces are no longer in line and the aircraft tends to slide or slip sideways.

Small amounts of sideslip have little or no effect without dihedral, but when dihedral is present, the angle of attack of the wing on the 'into slip' side is increased and that on the up side reduced. An imbalance appears, tending to tilt the wing (Figure 5.16 and compare Figure 2.9). This can be visualised by viewing a model with dihedral from in front and slightly to one side. The line of sight then represents the direction of the airflow striking the wing, and the increased angle of attack of the 'into slip' wing is at once obvious. The resulting roll is a direct result of this angular change.

Several complicating factors arise. When the wing is banked, the sideways tilting of the lift force begins to turn the aircraft. Tilting the lift force reduces the upward support, so this no longer equals the weight and changes the fore-aft balance. The aircraft thus tends to pitch slightly nose down and lose height. Also, during the sideslip, the normal weathercocking stability of the model will yaw it towards the slip. Thus a simple lateral disturbance causes rotations about all three axes of the aeroplane.

The dihedral comes into play so long as the slip continues. A further important effect enters here. When a wing, or any part of it, is operated at an increased angle of attack, the energy of the tip vortex becomes greater and this increases the drag. The dihedral causes the wing on the down side to lift more strongly than on the other side so the vortex drag also increases on the down side wing (now lifting more strongly) and decreases on the other wing. The lift difference corrects the bank but tends to yaw the model as it does so. Two effects combine. The vertical stabilisers yaw the aeroplane into the airflow, and the vortex drag reinforces this yaw. If the dihedral is too great, the vortex drag may actually yaw the model too far and then the vertical stabilisers come into play in the opposite direction. The combined effects often tend to produce a good deal of oscillation in both yaw and roll before the model settles down again. The matching of vertical stabiliser areas to dihedral is often quite difficult and requires experiment to achieve a satisfactory combination.

As with all other forms of stability, a model stable in roll will hold a banked attitude when required to do so. It should be remembered that banking, tilting the wing lift force to one side, will turn the aircraft. A wing with dihedral will behave in just the same way when the model is trimmed for a steady turn, as when it is in level flight. That is, it will tend to return the aircraft to the required angle of bank, and hence, rate of turn, after a disturbance. A model in a correctly flown turn will have no sideslip or skidding. The mass of the model, resisting the turn, produces inertia forces. The effect of these is to tilt the total mass reaction in turning flight, so that it exactly opposes the total lift. Both forces act at right angles to the crosswise or Y axis of the model. (To provide the increase in lift required, the elevator has to bring the mainplane to a higher angle of attack than for level flight, and slightly more power may be required from the motor to maintain the airspeed, in the turn.) The resulting balance of forces continues as long as the correct angle of bank and elevator trim are held. If, now, a gust tilts the wing to some different angle, either increasing the bank or decreasing it, the balance is disturbed, and either a slip or a skid, into or out of, the turn, results. If the wing has dihedral, the unbalanced lift forces will tend to tilt the wing back to the original angle of bank. This is a stable reaction. Dihedral does not, therefore, automatically bring a model back to straight and level, but tends to hold it in a turn if it is trimmed for turning, and holds it straight and level if it is trimmed for straight and level. This is exactly what is required.

Many aircraft with little or no dihedral are to some extent spirally unstable. In a turn, if left alone, the angle of bank gradually increases and the aircraft enters a spiralling descent. If no corrective action is taken, this steepens to become a spiral dive. The build up of the spiral is fairly gradual and can be corrected by the pilot without much difficulty as a rule.

In inverted flight, dihedral operates the other way round. A sideslip to one side causes a roll towards that side, and unless corrected by the pilot, the model will fall over into the normal, upright position. Hence, models with dihedral are not stable for inverted flight. For this reason, aerobatic models rarely have dihedral, the competent pilot preferring neutral stability in both senses to stability in one sense and instability in the other. (Note the effect of sweepback, 5.12, below.)

5.11 Holding off bank

As mentioned in Chapter 2, if a model, such as a sailplane, has a large span in relation to its wing area and weight (low span loading and high aspect ratio), when the aircraft is in a turn the outer wing tends to produce more lift than the one on the inner side of the turn. This is because the outer wing is following a longer path through the air, tending to steepen the bank. Many sailplanes require the ailerons to be set slightly against the turn. The effect is hardly noticeable in the ordinary, short span, low aspect ratio powered model, because the radius of turning flight is much greater, relative to the span. The difference of flow speed over the inner and outer wings is almost negligible.

5.12 Sweep effects

Sweep back has a stabilising effect in roll similar to dihedral. If the aircraft is banked by a gust, a slip towards the lower wing begins. Since the wing is swept back, the angle of attack presented by the low wing is greater than that of the other and a corresponding difference of lift arises, tending to roll the aircraft back to its previous position. This may be visualised by viewing a swept back wing from in front and slightly to one side, as for the dihedral effect.

This characteristic of sweep back is valuable since, unlike dihedral, it operates both right way up and inverted. An aerobatic model aircraft may thus be given some positive roll stability in both conditions, whereas dihedral stabilises only for the upright attitude.

The disadvantage of sweepback appears at low speeds, when the model is coming in to land, for example. A swept back wing tends to stall at the tips first, so caution is needed to prevent accidents during the low speed phase of flight.

Sweep forward has the opposite effects, and is equivalent to anhedral, de-stabilising the aeroplane in roll, and improving low speed control. In some military aircraft with pronounced sweepback, the wings are given anhedral to render the aircraft less stable, and hence more responsive, in the rolling sense.

6   THE PROPELLER

6.1 Propeller basics

A propeller converts rotational power or torque from the engine into thrust to move the aeroplane forward. Turbines, including wind, water and gas turbines, are very similar in principle but their function is to extract power from a fluid flow and convert it into torque. They work like propellers in reverse and are shaped accordingly.

A propeller is best thought of as a rotating system of wing-like blades (Figure 6.1). The most important features are the area of the *disc* swept by the blades as they rotate, the number of blades, their *angle of attack* and their *shape* and *cross section*. These in turn determine the *lift and drag* forces on the blades and hence the propeller's efficiency as a converter of engine torque to thrust.

6.2 Diameter

The diameter of the disc swept by the propeller, sometimes called the *actuator disc*, determines the quantity or mass of air available for the blades to work on, in each unit of time (Figure 6.2). The propeller produces thrust by drawing in a mass of air from in front and accelerating

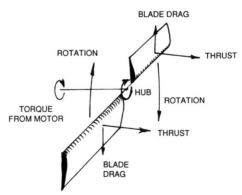

Figure 6.1 The propeller as a system of rotating wings. (Such 'paddle' type propellers are sometimes used for indoor models)

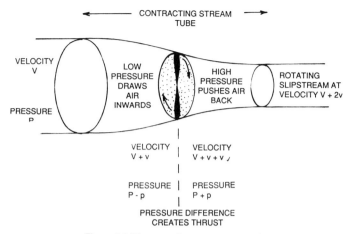

Figure 6.2 The propeller as an actuator disc

it through the swept disc to a higher velocity. The result of this acceleration is a reaction force on the blades which is transmitted to the hub and thence to the aircraft.

There is a low pressure area in front of the disc. Air ahead of the propeller senses the pressure reduction and begins to accelerate towards the disc before the propeller arrives. As the flow passes through the disc, there is a large increase in pressure over the whole disc area, so the air flows rapidly away in a relatively narrow *slipstream*. Half the increase of slipstream flow speed occurs in front of the disc, on the low pressure side, and half behind the disc, on the high pressure side. The thrust produced is the total of the pressure difference between front and back of the disc, which in turn relates to the increase of momentum produced in the air as it passes through.

The reality of the slipstream flow in front of the propeller may be confirmed by watching small pieces of dust or grass being drawn into the disc from in front of a model standing on the ground with engine running. (The danger of a model flier's tie being allowed to dangle in front of the propeller when starting the engine is well known. The air flowing in towards the disc may take the tie into the blades with it.)

In each moment, as much air must leave the disc as flows in. Since the velocity of the flow increases, the slipstream ahead of the blades contracts inwards and this contraction continues for some distance behind, producing a *stream tube* of reduced cross section and high velocity. Because the blades of the propeller create drag, the slipstream rotates as it flows aft. (The effects of this rotation on the vertical tail surfaces of most models has been noted in earlier chapters.)

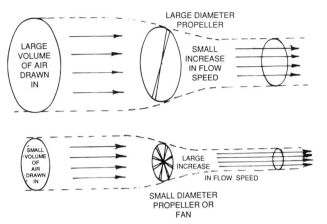

Figure 6.3 Other things equal, large diameter
propellers are more efficient than small ones

Supposing that the power input is the same in each case (which is rarely so in practice), a propeller of small diameter may produce the same thrust as a larger one, but only if the propeller turns at a higher speed, and/or has a larger number of blades. The alternatives are to act on a large mass of air and give it a relatively gentle acceleration, spread over a large disc area, or to seize a smaller mass of air and accelerate it to a higher velocity. A small pressure difference spread over a large area gives as much thrust as a large pressure difference over a small disc area. The fan or ducted fan power unit represents one extreme in model flying. In this, a relatively small mass of air is drawn into the fan, which has many blades turning at a high rate. There is a large pressure difference between front and rear of the fan, over a small disc. (The ducted fan unit lends itself to scale models of jet aircraft because of its small diameter.) At the other extreme, a helicopter rotor sweeping a large disc acts on large masses of air but accelerates them relatively little to obtain the reaction.

At model flying speeds, the most efficient use of power is yielded by working on the largest possible mass of air and accelerating it gently. In other words, large diameter propellers are aerodynamically more efficient than small ones (Figure 6.3). There are, unfortunately, many practical limitations on the diameter of model propellers. The tips must be kept clear of the ground during take off and landing runs. The larger the propeller diameter, the longer the undercarriage of the aeroplane must be, unless a very unusual layout, perhaps with the power unit in a pod on a high pylon, is used. Both long undercarriages and tall pylon mountings present great difficulties, not least their high aerodynamic drag, weight and inherent vulnerability to damage.

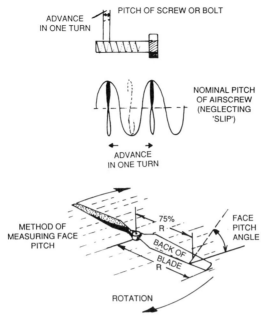

ADVANCE IN ONE TURN

PITCH OF SCREW OR BOLT

NOMINAL PITCH OF AIRSCREW (NEGLECTING 'SLIP')

ADVANCE IN ONE TURN

METHOD OF MEASURING FACE PITCH

75% R

FACE PITCH ANGLE

BACK OF BLADE R

ROTATION

Figure 6.4 Propeller pitch

In addition, the forces on a propeller blade when it is turning are quite powerful. A large diameter propeller may run into trouble if the blades twist or flutter. Blades sometimes break under load. Every increase in diameter increases these difficulties and the usual solution is to compromise with a propeller of moderate diameter. Given the choice between a large and small diameter propeller, to obtain the greatest thrust from a given torque, the larger propeller should be used.

6.3 Pitch

A propeller is sometimes called an *airscrew* because it seems to screw its way through the fluid in a manner resembling a screw or bolt. Along with this idea goes the notion of *pitch,* which is analogous to the distance advanced by a screw in one complete turn. The pitch of a propeller is usually expressed as a distance in centimetres or inches.

When propellers are sold in model shops, the pitch and diameter are always stated and the difference between different pitches may best be observed by a comparison of several of the same diameter. In the first instance, pitch and diameter should be chosen to match the engine used, following the recommendation of the engine manufacturer or an experienced model flier. With some understanding of how propellers work, however, it is usually possible to make improvements.

The nominal pitch does not give a true picture of how far the propeller advances at each revolution. The actual advance is always less. This has led to the idea of propeller *slip*. What this represents is not any slippage of the propeller blades, but the *angle of attack of the blades* to the airflow in which they operate (Figure 6.5).

Taking any small section of a propeller blade, it can produce thrust only if it approaches the air in its immediate neighbourhood at some positive aerodynamic angle of attack. Since the air is flowing through the propeller disc at some speed, the angle of attack of the blade depends not only on its own speed, due to rotation, and its pitch, but on the speed of the flow through the disc. In flight this is related to the airspeed of the model, but a model held on the ground with engine running before take off will also draw air in from in front and thrust is produced in the same way as in flight. (Note that, because half the stream tube velocity is due to air accelerating towards the propeller disc, the flow speed through the disc in flight is not the same as the flight speed of the model, but greater. A propeller turning when the model is standing still produces thrust because it draws air in and accelerates it aftwards. A propeller in flight does exactly the same; it makes no difference to the thrust produced if the air is thought of as flowing through the disc, or if the disc is thought of as moving forward. In the same way, a wing fixed in a wind tunnel with a flow passing over it produces the same lift as it would if it were a wing passing through the air at the same speed and angle of attack. The total thrust of the propeller is the product of the pressure difference between front and back of the propeller disc in all conditions.)

Just as with a wing section, the angle of incidence (i.e., the angle to the propeller disc) of the propeller blade at some point along the radius may be measured in degrees. Most propeller aerofoil sections

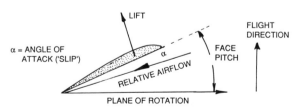

THE TRUE MEANING OF 'SLIP'

Figure 6.5 The so-called 'slip' of a propeller is actually the blade angle of attack relative to the air

have at least some portion of their rear face flat, and the custom has grown up of using the flat, or nearly flat, part of the blade section as the reference for pitch measurements. Some pitch gauges sold commercially, or made at home, rely on this convention. This, however, gives different results, depending on differences between the aerofoil sections used on different propellers (see Chapter 3.8). If instead of the flat face of the blade being used, pitch measurements were made from the true chord line of the aerofoil, the pitch figure would be larger than the face or nominal pitch. If the blade aerofoil sections differ slightly, as they usually do, identical pitches measured from the rear face will be different if measured from the true chord. The result is that no exact comparison of pitches on commercially available propellers is possible.

A third possibility is to measure pitch from the *aerodynamic zero* of the blade aerofoil section (Figure 6.6). It was explained in 3.10 that any aerofoil section has some angle of attack at which it produces zero lift. Strictly, it makes more sense to measure pitch from this angle rather than from the geometric chord line. This, however, is never done in aeromodelling, partly because the characteristics of the propeller blade aerofoils are not accurately known.

6.4 The constant pitch propeller
However pitch is measured, the airflow through the disc moves a certain distance during each revolution, although this distance is not normally the same as the nominal pitch. At the tip of a rotating propeller, the blade travels very rapidly around the circumference of the actuator disc. The direction of the airflow meeting the blade at this point is the product of the stream tube flow velocity and the high blade rotational velocity. Nearer to the hub, the rotational speed of the blade is lower, but the stream tube velocity is (approximately) the same as at the tip. If it is required that the blade at every place from root to tip should meet the relative airflow at the same *angle of attack,* the blade must be given a *helical* twist. The result is a *constant pitch* propeller.

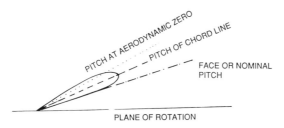

Figure 6.6 Three ways of measuring propeller pitch

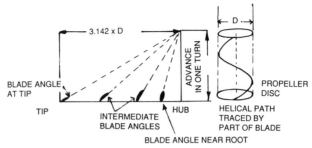

**Figure 6.7 Layout of blade angles
for constant pitch [D = propeller diameter]**

The tip section is inclined at a small angle to the disc, while the root end is at a greater angle. At the centre, the blade would theoretically have to be at 90 degrees to the disc, but this point is occupied by the propeller hub so the blade terminates before reaching it (Figure 6.7).

In practice, most commercially manufactured model propellers, although approximating the helical twist, are not perfectly constant in pitch. This is partly because of the difficulties of measuring the pitch in the first place. Most propeller blades require considerable thickening and stiffening towards their root ends, to withstand the stresses there. The blade section changes progressively from a thin section at the tip to a thicker one half way in along the radius, to a very thick profile near the hub. While constant pitch may be arranged over the outer parts of the blade, the inner ends tend to depart considerably from this.

It is also sometimes useful to give a propeller blade the equivalent of washout, which entails twisting the outer blade to a lower pitch angle than the inner sections. Another reason for the different behaviour of nominally similar propellers is that they may depart to greater or smaller degrees from the constant pitch geometry.

Yet another difficulty in comparing propellers now arises. If the blade is of constant pitch, wherever the pitch is measured along the blade, from root to tip, will produce the same figure because the helical

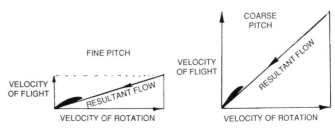

Figure 6.8 Fine and coarse propeller pitch

twist of the blades is designed precisely for this result. If, however, the blade is not of constant pitch, a different figure will appear, depending on which radial point along the blade is used for the measurement. Some manufacturers measure the pitch at about two-thirds of the way along the blade. Others use a different station. With non-helically twisted blades, this results in different nominal pitch figures for the identical blade. It is the nominal pitch that the manufacturer marks on the product, measured by whatever convention that manufacturer prefers.

This does not imply that the constant pitch propeller is always more efficient than one with non-constant pitch. The constant pitch angles are laid out for one flight velocity only. The propeller will produce a constant angle of attack along its whole length only when the flow speed through the actuator disc is exactly what was assumed. At any other speed, the angles will be different. The constant pitch propeller gives its best performance at the one speed for which it is designed. A long distance transport aircraft, for instance, apart from take off and landing, flies at an almost constant airspeed and requires a constant pitch propeller set for this speed. The non-constant pitch propeller does not reach any sharp peak of efficiency but is capable of operating effectively with an aircraft which varies speed in flight a great deal, like an aerobatic model.

6.5 Coarse and fine pitch

When an aeroplane is flying very fast, the flight speed ensures that the air arriving at the actuator disc is moving very rapidly and the propeller blades then need to be set at a large angle to the plane of rotation if they are to meet this fast flow at a reasonable angle. Such a propeller will have *coarse pitch.* When the flight speed is slow, the propeller blades should be set at a smaller angle to the disc, that is, at *fine pitch* (Figure 6.8).

The fine pitch propeller is particularly useful when the aircraft is accelerating from standstill to take off speed, but once airborne, tends to restrict the maximum attainable airspeed. The blade angles of attack to the air become too small. A coarse pitch propeller of large diameter may overload the engine so much that take off speed, is never reached. The blades of such a propeller may stall when full power is applied to get the aeroplane moving. Reducing either pitch or diameter will improve the situation. Experience with models and engines of similar size and speed is the best guide for making the choice of pitch, but experiment with different types of propeller is necessary to get the most from any model.

Although rarely seen on a model aircraft, the *variable pitch* propeller should be mentioned. In this, the blades are capable of being rotated at the hub to different pitch angles. This enables the pilot to choose a fine pitch when the aircraft is moving slowly through the air, or a coarse pitch for high speed flight. Fine pitch is selected for the accelerating ground run before take off, since when the aeroplane is at rest, the flow speed through the propeller disc is slow. Fine pitch is also used for climbing steeply when the power requirements are large but, because of the climb, airspeed is slow.

6.6 Blade lift and thrust

The lift produced by a blade is not all available as thrust (Figure 6.9). Blade lift acts at right angles to the local airflow direction, not to the plane of the propeller disc. The lift force therefore is inclined somewhat backwards relative to the direction of flight. Some of the lift resists the rotation, increasing the drag.

Near the tip of the blade, the rotational speed is high in relation to the velocity of the flow through the disc. Hence at this point the blade is set at such an angle to the disc that most of its lift is directed forwards as thrust. Near the hub, the blade is moving round relatively slowly and the local direction of the airflow is dominated by the stream tube velocity from fore to aft. The blade here must be set at a greater angle to the disc, and most of the lift force acts against the rotation.

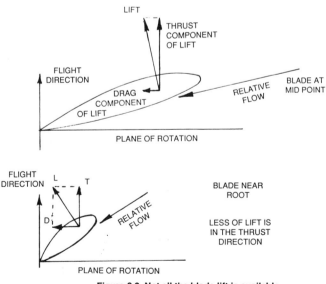

Figure 6.9 Not all the blade lift is available as thrust. A proportion of the lift force resists the torque

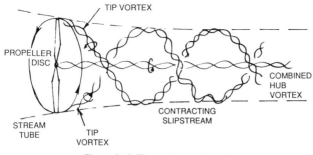

Figure 6.10 The vortex system of a two
bladed propeller

Little is available as thrust. The outer parts of a propeller blade are more effective, from the thrust viewpoint, than the inner parts.

6.7 The propeller vortex system

Every blade of a propeller produces a vortex at both ends, root and tip, because there is a tendency for air to flow from the high pressure side of the blade to the low pressure side, as at a wing tip. The vortices create drag, representing wasted power.

The tip vortex trails behind the blade and conforms to the contracting diameter of the stream tube behind the actuator disc. Behind the propeller, therefore, is a system of trailing vortices, one vortex from each blade, which may be thought of as twisted round the outer limits of the slipstream (Figure 6.10).

At the inner end of the blade, because the flow velocities are smaller and the pressure differences between the face and back of the blade are less, the vortex is less powerful, but it exists. Since the dominant flow direction is from fore to aft, this inner vortex trails almost directly downstream. It unites with the vortices produced by the other blades. In most ordinary 'tractor' type aeroplanes, the presence of a fuselage and, usually, an engine cooling arrangement of some kind, immediately behind the propeller hub, restricts the hub vortices from their full development, but they none the less do exist and represent additional drag and wastage of engine power. If there is a spinner to fair the propeller hub the vortices from the blades twist themselves around the fuselage and unite into one behind the model.

6.8 Blade interference

Air being a fluid, every change of pressure and flow in one place is communicated in all directions to other places nearby. A propeller blade, with its tip and hub vortices, induces downwash in front and behind, so distorting the airflow everywhere ahead of, and behind, the propeller disc. As a blade moves round, it necessarily comes into air which has been downwashed by the blade ahead of it, and in its turn, it disturbs the air behind for the next blade. The effect is very similar to the interference between the forewing and rear wing of a tandem aeroplane.

Even a single blade works in the downwash created by itself as it passed through on previous rotations. This type of interference becomes more pronounced as the number of blades increases. Single bladed propellers are used on free flight, rubber driven model aeroplanes. They are slightly more efficient aerodynamically than two or more bladed forms because the air in which they work is less disturbed. (They have to be counterbalanced to permit them to turn smoothly. The presence of the rotating counterweight tends to increase propeller drag to some extent, so the full benefit is not gained.) The most usual type of two bladed propeller is on the whole more practical, since the blades balance one another and although there is mutual interference the losses are not very large. As the number of blades multiplies, the interference increases, so that it is not possible to obtain the same thrust efficiency with a large number of blades as with a single one, even if the propellers are turning at the same speed.

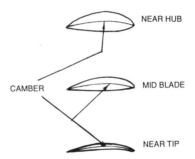

Figure 6.11 Blade section changes along
the blade may not affect camber

6.9 Blade sections

The aerofoil sections used for propeller blades are essentially similar to those used for wings. They are usually cambered (Figure 6.11). The structural necessity for the blade to be strong at the hub end requires the section to be thicker there than at the tip. If the tip section mean line camber (see 3.8 above) is continued all the way to the root of the blade, the aerofoil profile will change from a thin, possibly 'undercambered' form at the tip to an approximately 'flat bottomed' section somewhere further in, to a 'semi symmetrical' shape nearer the hub. These terms, as noted before, are very misleading since the camber may in fact be the same in each case.

The flow conditions in the boundary layer of a propeller blade are very complex. As the propeller rotates, centrifugal forces acting on the layer of air which is most closely in contact with the surface of the blade tend to force the flow outwards towards the tips. The air above this innermost layer is less attached to the blade and so does not feel the centrifugal force so strongly. This diminishing effect continues outwards through the boundary layer. Hence, within the boundary layer itself, cross flows develop and tiny vortices form. These practically exclude the possibility of any laminar flow occurring in the boundary layer. Little benefit is found if the aerofoil section of a propeller is replaced by a low drag, laminar flow form. In practice, model aeroplane propeller aerofoils are of a relatively simple kind, with small camber, and there are frequently more or less arbitrary changes of section along the blade.

6.10 Blade shape

As with a wing, the most efficient propeller blade is one which produces the least vortex drag and this can be achieved with a correct layout of the blade in plan. Since the blade is twisted, the planform can be determined only by projecting, or 'unwinding' the blade in imagination to find the developed form. Because the blade moves faster through the air at the tip than at the root, the simple elliptical shape is not the best. If proper allowance is made for the blade speed variation radially, the propeller gives least vortex drag when the tip is considerably narrower, or more pointed, than the equivalent elliptical shape.

In practice, although keen contest modellers often modify blade shapes by carving or grinding away parts of the blade and re-balancing and polishing, typical commercial model propellers do not approach this ideal. Efficiency suffers, but the difference is not so great that it becomes of major concern for the sport flier. As with a wing, the difference between a blade shaped exactly to the ideal and one which approximates it fairly well is small. Propeller efficiency and correct blade shape proved of crucial importance to human-powered aircraft. The first propeller fitted to the MacCready *Gossamer Albatross* proved inadequate to sustain flight for more than a few minutes. With a new propeller designed by Eugene Larrabee, it crossed the English Channel.

6.11 Torque reaction

A propeller blade driven by an engine creates aerodynamic drag which resists the torque. This resistance, as usual in all fluid flow, increases with the square of the flow speed (twice the velocity, four times the reaction). Hence to make a given propeller turn faster, in order to provide more thrust, requires a relatively large increase of engine power.

The propeller blades' total drag reaction thus normally equals the engine's torque output. The aeroplane feels this reaction as a force tending to roll the model round the thrust axis, in the direction opposite to the propeller rotation (Figure 6.12). With engines normally turning clockwise when viewed from behind, the reaction is a rolling tendency to port. On the ground, this tends to throw more weight onto the left hand wheel or wheels of the undercarriage and this may cause a swing to that side on take of. In flight, there is often a need for some slight aileron trim to prevent the torque reaction pushing the left wing down.

6.12 The 'P' effect and gyroscopic forces

Two other forces of interest arise with propellers. The first of these, the so-called 'P' effect, is aerodynamic in character (Figure 6.13). If a propeller disc is inclined to the approaching airflow at some angle, as happens when the model is trimmed to fly nose up, or nose down, or sideslipping, instead of aligned truly with the airflow, the angle of attack of the blades on one side of the disc is greater than on the other. This causes the thrust force from the propeller to act slightly off centre, and this tends to yaw the model. This is not usually very noticeable but it increases the tendency to swing on take off with a tailwheeled undercarriage. In the early stages of the take off run, the model is tail down. The airflow thus comes at the propeller at a fairly marked angle and the 'P' effect encourages a leftward swing. This reinforces the torque effect mentioned above.

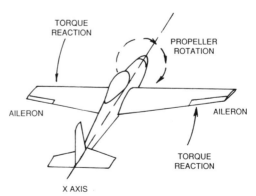

Figure 6.12 The torque reaction may require
aileron trim to balance rolling tendency

The *gyroscopic reaction* of a propeller is, strictly, not aerodynamic but mechanical (Figure 6.14). It does, however, work with the torque and 'P' effect to encourage left-handed swinging during take off. If a rotating wheel, or propeller, is forced to change the direction of its axis, it reacts powerfully and tends to align its axis at ninety degrees to the direction of the disturbing force. The most commonplace example of this is found in riding a bicycle. If, while rolling along, the bicycle tilts to the left, forcing the axle of the front wheel over that way, the gyroscopic reaction tends to force the handlebars round to the left. This, as every rider knows, helps to restore the balance and enables a bicycle to be ridden 'hands off' by deliberately tilting the machine to one side or the other in order to steer it.

A propeller responds in the same way. Viewed from the rear, the normal model propeller rotates clockwise. A 'tail dragging' aeroplane

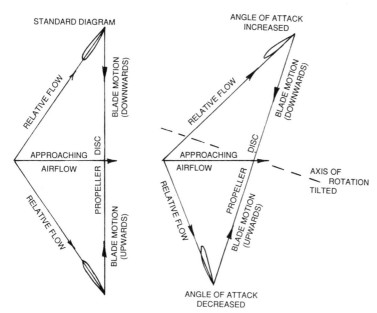

Figure 6.13 The 'P' effect (angles greatly exaggerated).
The standard diagram on the left assumes that the
propeller disc is square to the approaching flow.
Relative flow over both blades is the same.
When the propeller disc is tilted relative to the flow
(as during take off with a tailwheel undercarriage),
the relative flow angles to the blades are different.
The downgoing blade is at a higher angle of attack
than the upgoing blade. With a normal direction of
propeller rotation, more thrust is produced on the
right hand side, tending to aid a leftward swing.

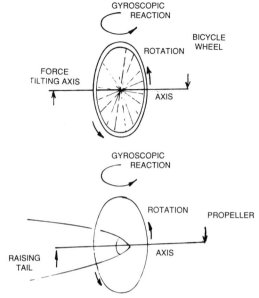

Figure 6.14 The gyroscopic reaction. Tilting the axis
of a rotating wheel, such as a bicycle wheel, produces
a powerful reaction tending to align the axis of
rotation at right angles to the disturbing force.
A propeller behaves in the same way. With normal
propeller rotation directions, raising the tail produces
a leftward swing.

during take off, at a certain forward speed, raises its tail. This causes
the axis of the propeller to tilt and the gyroscopic reaction is a leftward
swing.

There are thus four forces tending to make an aeroplane driven by
a normal, clockwise turning propeller, swing to the left during take off;
the torque reaction, the 'P' effect, the gyroscopic reaction and the
slipstream rotation striking the vertical tail, as mentioned in 2.3. The
'P' and gyroscopic forces are most noticeable with tailwheeled aircraft, but the torque and slipstream effects are found on tricycle undercarriage types as well. The pilot must be prepared to use the rudder to
counteract these tendencies, which do not entirely disappear when
the aircraft is off the ground.

INDEX

Reference numbers in the index refer to paragraph numbers in the text.